Enforcement in the EU Single Market

Jacques Pelkmans

AND

Anabela Correia de Brito

WITH A FOREWORD BY MALCOLM HARBOUR
CHAIRMAN, INTERNAL MARKET AND CONSUMER PROTECTION COMMITTEE
EUROPEAN PARLIAMENT

CENTRE FOR EUROPEAN POLICY STUDIES (CEPS)
BRUSSELS

The Centre for European Policy Studies (CEPS) is an independent policy research institute in Brussels. Its mission is to produce sound policy research leading to constructive solutions to the challenges facing Europe. The views expressed in this book are entirely those of the authors and should not be attributed to CEPS or any other institution with which they are associated or to the European Union.

This study was conducted for Nordic Innovation, an official organ of the Nordic Council of Ministers, and also served as an input for a parallel study conducted by CopenhagenEconomics during the Danish Presidency for Nordic Innovation. The authors are grateful for the permission given by Nordic Innovation and CopenhagenEconomics to publish their contribution.

Jacques Pelkmans is Senior Research Fellow at CEPS and Anabela Correia de Brito is a Research Fellow. The authors are grateful to Amarilys Verhoeven, Head of Unit responsible for the "Your Europe Advice" portal and the SOLVIT network at the European Commission and Anouska Janssens, team leader of SOLVIT at the European Commission, Giuseppe Casella, Head of Unit responsible for the notification of technical regulations at DG Enterprises, and Kamila Skowyra and Sigrid Brettel, both legal officers at DG Enterprises, for their helpful cooperation throughout the research.

TABLE OF CONTENTS

List of Figures

List of Tables

FOREWORD

My ambition to become a Member of the European Parliament was driven, to a large extent, by my enthusiasm for the Single European Market. As a commercial executive in a car company, I had experienced the day-to-day frustrations of non-tariff barriers and technical hurdles. I was outraged by the unproductive and unnecessary 'red tape' that strangled competition and consumer choice.

Since 2009, I have had the privilege of being Chairman of the European Parliament's leading committee on single market issues. I am pleased that, with support from across the political spectrum, we have been instrumental in re-launching the drive towards a better functioning market. The Single Market Act is the biggest political initiative to boost the market since 1992. In October 2012, we will be marking the 20th anniversary of the first Single Market programme. It is very timely, therefore, to welcome this invaluable work of reference and scholarship on the biggest issue still facing the single market, the enforcement of the rules creating a truly 'barrier-free' Europe.

In my experience, too little policy analysis is carried out on single market issues. For students of European politics, other topics (such as Treaty or Governance issues) always appear to be much more glamorous. But a thorough examination of the 'technology' of the single market and recommendations on the ways to make its 'mechanisms' work more smoothly and efficiently are surely essential if the potential gains in job creation, business start-ups, wealth generation and consumer choice are to be realised.

For many years, Professor Jacques Pelkmans has been a leader in research on the single market, and we started to share ideas soon after I was elected in 1999. He has continued to be at the forefront of intellectual single market advocacy. This book reinforces the case that my Committee makes every time we meet – weak enforcement and compliance are the biggest obstacles to reaping its full benefits.

Professor Pelkmans and Anabela Corriera de Brito add an in-depth analysis to the case that Parliament makes regularly: formal infringement procedures enforced by the Court of Justice of the European Union are time consuming, cumbersome and expensive. The focus must shift to non-legislative instruments, by better cooperation between administrations and by empowering affected stakeholders (including consumers, citizens, enterprises and public authorities) to challenge administrations where their rights are being infringed. Parliament has strongly supported SOLVIT, and just approved an enhancement of the Internal Market Information system, both instruments that are strongly endorsed by this book.

We are also deeply engaged in our examination of public procurement reforms, which we hope will deliver a framework that encourages competition and delivers better outcomes for citizens in the delivery of modern and more effective public services.

I hope that this book will command a wide audience, and stimulate more practical and effective enforcement tools that will unshackle the full potential of the single market.

Malcolm Harbour
MEP and Chairman of the Internal Market and Consumer Protection
Committee in the European Parliament
Brussels, September 2012

EXECUTIVE SUMMARY

Enforcement of and compliance with EU law, and in particular in the single market, are not only legally necessary but also of economic importance for business, consumers and the European economy at large. Only with reliable, permanent and effective enforcement will all the potential gains from the single market be fully reaped.

The present CEPS study provides an overview of classical infringement approaches and a range of new EU enforcement methods employed in the single market. As far as we know, no such wide-ranging study exists. Every effort was made, where possible, to keep the text accessible (and non-legalistic). We provide extensive empirical analysis and trends of practically all tools that are currently employed.

A broader, strategic view of EU enforcement distinguishes five critical aspects: i) good detection of bad implementation, a lack of implementation or bad or non-application; ii) formal infringement procedures (the classical route); iii) pre-infringement initiatives (ensuring that no infringement procedure will be necessary); iv) preventive initiatives and v) reduction of transaction and information costs when exploiting the single market rights or laws. The study pays ample attention to the first four.

Central to modern enforcement is the fact that the classical route to the Court of Justice of the European Union (CJEU) is costly and takes a lot of time. It is rarely suitable for European business confronted with suspected enforcement problems, let alone consumers. Of course, formal infringement procedures must always remain available for genuine issues of interpretation or, more generally, for the credibility of the system. But they will never yield a proper functioning single market in and by themselves and therefore have to be complemented by a host of other measures and initiatives.

Amongst the more important new instruments, the pre-infringement ones like SOLVIT and EU-Pilot have truly made a difference. SOLVIT is free of charge, easy to access (on-line) and has achieved an impressive record in terms of speed in handling cases (on average within 10 weeks) and successful resolution (around 90% of the cases). EU Pilot is a relatively informal mechanism operating between member states and the European Commission with a view to minimising infringement cases and doing this rapidly. Initiated only in 2008, it has quickly become quite effective.

At least as important, if not more so, are the preventive approaches, including e.g. the on-line inter-member state Internal Market Information (IMI) communication system between officials at national and regional level, which reduces transaction costs enormously, while enhancing trust between administrations and greatly increasing speed in many cases. The steady (selective) shift from directives to regulations for the internal market has also pre-empted numerous implementation problems, and the Directive 98/34 procedures have worked remarkably well in preventing new technical barriers from arising in the single market.

Our study leads to a series of recommendations, of which the more important ones include:

- Despite the recent more effective enforcement in the single market, it would be a mistake to hold that the enforcement issue is 'solved', far from it.
- A successful EU enforcement strategy should not primarily be legal in nature, but pay explicit attention to factors such as the right incentives (or the absence of disincentives) for complainants, speed of resolution, resources (e.g. for SOLVIT) and the benefit/cost ratio of detection and resolution mechanisms.
- Member states' active and willing cooperation is and will remain the key to effective enforcement.
- Success stories include SOLVIT, EU Pilot, the Internal Market Scoreboard, the mutual recognition Regulation 764/2008 and preventing new technical barriers via the Directive 98/34 procedure.
- Among all types of EU single market legislation, the problems with public procurement are undoubtedly the harder ones. The potential market is huge: there is still an enormous potential of cross-border competition for contracts and the economic welfare gains can be very substantial. The European Commission's proposals of December 2011 should be of some help. There should be more harmonisation, including in the national review and remedies systems.

1. Introduction

Proper enforcement of EU law in the single market is as crucial as enacting the EU laws in the first place. In business circles and, at times, amongst consumers, there are lingering doubts about the effectiveness of enforcement of single market laws, including case law of the Court of Justice of the European Union (CJEU). These doubts cause frustration, higher costs (than necessary under EU law) and missed opportunities for European business, as well as reduced confidence amongst consumers in selected goods and services. Such frustrations or anxieties may also play a role in the temporary provision of cross-border services (by 'posted workers') or with specific forms of establishment in some services sectors. The result is that the single market does not function properly.

However, the value-added of the single market has been, right from the beginning of the EU in 1958, precisely its potential to generate economic growth, *in addition to* what a single EU country could ever achieve alone, through 'ever-deeper market integration' over a large economic space. Nowadays, even more than ever before in 55 years of EU history, companies are keen to exploit the manifold single market opportunities as much as possible as a rare source of growth in times of shrinking demand and an austere fiscal stance by almost all EU governments. Apart from breaking down or otherwise overcoming barriers to market access by means of the Single Market Act, it is also important to maximise the effectiveness of free movement in the single market, to encourage unhindered establishment in other EU countries and to strengthen the enforcement of EU law.

This study is an attempt to identify existing 'enforcement barriers', to survey the entire spectrum of efforts to improve enforcement or to pre-empt infringement in the first place as well as to provide and rework recent empirical data facilitating the development of an economic assessment of internal market enforcement efforts and their potential.

Chapter 2 will define and 'confine' the notion of 'enforcement barriers' in the broader context of 'enforcement failures', followed by a brief note on a 'typology' of enforcement barriers (chapter 3). Chapter 4 surveys the spectrum of EU enforcement efforts consisting of five areas of activity at EU and member state level: i) detection of (possible) infringements of EU law, ii) pre-infringement procedure activities, iii) formal infringement procedures, iv) preventive measures and v) measures reducing transaction and information costs (mostly) for business. Chapters 5 through 8 consist of charting four areas of enforcement activity in some detail ('detection' will not be elaborated, except very briefly in chapter 4).

We have made an effort to employ non-legalistic language wherever possible, hopefully rendering the text more accessible to business persons and consumers. However, since our assignment also specified the need to incorporate a legal analysis, there will also be sections with a more elaborate legal character, in particular where it matters most, namely, for formal infringement procedures (chapter 6). Throughout this report, we have inserted a considerable amount of relevant empirical data. It should be realised there are data limitations as well as difficulties about the exact meaning of some of the data concerned with what business perceives as 'barriers'. We also will suggest in chapter 10 a number of concrete policy recommendations addressed to both the EU and the member state levels with a view to further facilitating the exploitation of the single market, in particular for goods.

2. DEFINING AND CONFINING 'ENFORCEMENT BARRIERS'

2.1 About 'barriers' and enforcement of single market law

When business wishes to engage in cross-border economic activities inside the single market, it may perceive or discern all kinds of 'barriers'. European business clearly remains suspicious or sceptical about the legal removal of barriers via EU laws as well as about enforcement of the four free movements and the right of establishment. More often than not, there is an attitude bordering on 'disbelief' in the effectiveness of complaining about perceived 'barriers'. Even recently, the European Business Test Panel (EBTP)[1] found that:

i)   29% of those doing cross-border intra-EU business are of the view that public authorities are not open to foreign business and are not responsive to their needs.

ii)   38% believe public authorities are not accessible and information regarding cross-border business is not transparent.

iii)   55% encounter a high level of administrative burdens.

iv)   39% think there is discrimination between national and foreign business.[2]

---

[1] European Commission Business Test Panel (2011), "Help us identify business obstacles in the Internal Market" (http://ec.europa.eu/yourvoice/ebtp/consultations/2011/obstacles/index_en.htm).

[2] The EBTP has developed a large network of businesses in touch with DG MARKT of the European Commission via occasional on-line consultations on various EU topics. For the present purpose, 440 companies responded. These were selected to ensure that all 27 EU countries were covered and that all business sizes and a wide range of sectors were represented.

This scepticism is not always based on sound knowledge of or even elementary insights into EU enforcement at national and EU level. Most businesses, except for the largest ones, simply do not take or have time for such 'non-productive' efforts, the effect of which is exactly to reinforce the sceptical view in business circles where many other colleagues tend to maintain similar, but untested, perspectives. This contribution aims to sketch the wide and gradually more effective landscape of enforcement actions at national and EU levels (and, indeed, jointly) and concentrate on facts, empirical measurement and qualitative evidence where relevant. The presumably overly sceptical perceptions in business circles will thus not be addressed, but this does not mean that they do not matter. They do matter, if only because a better appreciation amongst businesses of the many possibilities for enforcing EU law in the single market, most of them not involving any financial costs to companies, would lead to a much larger stream of complaints or notifications, in turn eventually generating a better functioning of the single market for businesses and consumers alike.

For entrepreneurs and managers, a 'barrier' to cross-border activities could be any legal or bureaucratic restriction or, for that matter 'illegal' restriction (under EU law), that hinders, renders more costly or throttles their business plans. Of course, business understands that some of these costs or restrictions may be justified (under EU law) and therefore merely have to be incorporated in their cross-border strategies and calculations. Ideally, European business would simply like to be informed in time and deal with these obligations as part of their preparations for cross-border business. In this ideal scenario, public requirements are precisely known and information is relevant and tailor-made to their business. Thus, in the eyes of business, a 'barrier' would be easy to recognise and it should be plain and basically costless to separate the 'justified' barriers (justified in the EU public interest) from the ones that are 'illegal' or, in any event, overly cumbersome, onerous and seemingly hard to justify.

In the EU of 2012, we do not live in such an ideal scenario and, indeed, we might never. It takes good and experienced (EU and national) market institutions and considerable administrative, networking and judicial efforts as well as agile and professional administrations that are open and helpful to business (and consumers when relevant) in order to minimise the presence of unjustified 'barriers' and their costs. In this study, the status quo of EU law and case law (the *acquis communautaire*) is taken as a given. Given the *acquis*, the question asked is whether it can be made to work for the proper functioning of the single market in a static as well as a dynamic sense. This requires *enforcement*: for the present purposes, the term 'enforcement' comprises all activities, public and private, at EU and member state level, to ensure the proper transposition of EU law into national law, proper implementation and the best possible application of EU law governing the single market everywhere in the Union – and the European Economic Area (EEA).

It should be realised that good enforcement cannot be taken for granted, for the simple reason that it is demanding. There is a well-developed literature in law, political science and public administration providing many reasons why enforcement may fail, be weak, remain underdeveloped or is selective.[3] Without pretending to provide a survey of this literature, we just consider reasons such as the bad 'fit' in national regulation as it existed before, the inherent problems of a certain EU regulation or directive (some EU laws are internally inconsistent or can be characterised as 'bad' regulation), capacity and interpretation issues in a national administration, the neglect of European standards linked to the relevant directive(s) and a lack of specialised expertise for highly technical directives (not least, their technical annexes or e.g. type-approval issues). The 'gold-plating' of directives in national law causing the requirements for business to be more onerous than justified by EU law also contributes to increased legal heterogeneity and uncertainty. Other times, the lack of or bad enforcement of EU law is connected with heavy-handed bureaucratic traditions (irrespective of what EU law really requires), domestic political frictions about some EU law and the lack of political legitimacy on a specific directive in domestic politics (rare, but disturbing when it does appear).

This list is far from exhaustive. Also note that it does not even include the motive of a 'protectionist' government. Broadly speaking, by now, member states are accustomed to EU law and know that intra-EU protectionism, even when covert, is neither correct nor easy to achieve, given enforcement. Today's acceptance of the rigour of the internal market is greater than ever before and this is a significant, although 'invisible' accomplishment. Nevertheless, there is always a temptation for some governments to be protectionist at the margin (especially before elections) or in the form of creating bureaucratic nuisance.

---

[3] Prominent examples from this literature include Siedentopf & Ziller (1988), Boerzel (2001 and 2002), Egan (2011), Falkner & Treib (2008), Guimaraes et al. (2010) and Mastenbroek (2005).

Business in Europe is entitled to benefit from good enforcement. The profound and lasting incentives of doing business in a large single market with many business customers and 500 million high-income consumers should only be mitigated by fully justified regulation, which is proportional (i.e. least-cost), fit-for-purpose and enforced or executed with the least-possible bureaucratic hindrances. Business would expect a high degree of transparency and predictability, so that it can anticipate or address whatever costs or quality adjustments or marketing questions such regulation and execution of rules might imply. In other words, no more costs than necessary, no unreasonable delays and no 'surprises' due to arbitrary discretion on the part of national administrations. Given currently prevailing EU regulation (and other relevant EU policies such as competition policy), the ideal single market should have no 'barriers' unless they are *justified, least-cost, transparent and predictable*. Surely, European business can live with such 'barriers' and will integrate them into their business plans together with numerous other business aspects of producing or marketing 'elsewhere'.

Would this ideal scenario mean that business would no longer complain about 'barriers' in the single market? The answer is: no, for two reasons: 'incompleteness' of the single market and 'national regulatory autonomy'. First, even in the ideal scenario, some 'barriers' will remain simply because member states have not yet tackled them, for reasons of lack of consensus (e.g. GMOs are the archetypical example) or because common minimum regulation has not received priority (e.g. private security services, after having been removed from the draft services Directive) or because EU regulation (and, sometimes, supervision) has addressed barriers but in an incomplete manner (e.g. even far-reaching financial services regulation does not yet cover mortgages in such a way as to arrive at a single market, not even in the eurozone where exchange rate risks are zero).

Second, member states retain regulatory autonomy in a range of issues or domains and they tend to jealously guard this autonomy for domestic political legitimacy reasons. The upshot is that, if business opportunities in domain X are partly or wholly governed by this national regulatory autonomy, companies are likely to encounter 'regulatory heterogeneity' amongst the 27 EU countries. In many instances, the differences in such national regulatory regimes do not reflect deeply-felt 'preferences' (like with GMOs) – that is, 'diversity', which ought to be respected in a union like the EU – but rather are merely the result of fragmented decision-making without any pressure or discipline to arrive at identical or even equivalent outcomes throughout the Union. This residual regulatory heterogeneity is costly to business and ultimately to customers and consumers, but it can only be reduced on a voluntary basis.

In this respect, the continuous European standardisation forms one route to achieve a gradual, almost invisible reduction of such heterogeneity costs, since some 18,000-plus of the 22,000 European standards are *not* connected to EU regulation, but amount to purely voluntary agreements to smoothen and improve the working of markets in Europe (and beyond perhaps). Such European standards automatically imply that national standards with the same purpose must be removed or withdrawn, which contributes to greater similarity in the functioning of (national) markets. Unfortunately, there are no other established paths to minimise regulatory heterogeneity, and many national constituencies may not even be interested to 'Europeanise' their rules voluntarily.

2.2   Enforcement failures: Barriers and distortions

This report focuses solely on *enforcement barriers*. In light of the above, we can now define more precisely what such barriers do and do not entail. Enforcement barriers take current EU law as a given. Thus, enforcement barriers are *not* about lingering obstacles to free movement or establishment, which have not been harmonised (hence, causing blockages or hindrances) and are *not* about higher costs due to national regulatory heterogeneity, even though business might perceive these as barriers to market access. Given the status quo in terms of EU law, *enforcement barriers* are strictly and only about bad or non-implementation or bad or non-application or bad or non-enforcement of EU law. In theory, the European Commission itself could perhaps fail to fulfil its crucial role as 'guardian of the treaties' and so generate enforcement barriers, but in actual practice this is so far-fetched, most of the time, that we shall ignore it. Enforcement barriers are, in reality, about failures of *member states* to properly apply and enforce EU law, including notably the single market *acquis*. Member states have several roles in the EU system, such as ratifying (or not) amendments to the treaties and agreeing (in Council) about EU legislation, but they are also 'agents' of the Union in ensuring that EU law is properly applied and enforced. Indeed, Art. 4 TEU and Art. 291, TFEU make this very clear.[4]

---

[4] Art. 4 TEU states that member states "shall take any appropriate measure, general or particular, to ensure fulfilment of the obligations arising out of the Treaties or

It follows that European business can count on the proper implementation of EU law into domestic law and, subsequently, its enforcement. If and when a member state fails to do this or does it inadequately, enforcement barriers will arise. When goods, services, workers, independents and securities move over intra-EU borders, local laws should, insofar as EU rules (and CJEU case law) are concerned, be identical or equivalent with respect to objectives and relevant instruments, whilst no provisions inconsistent with such laws or frustrating their explicit intent should remain on the books. Failure to ensure this can create difficulties for European business on the export side (via free movement), on the establishment side (for independents and for foreign direct investment), but also on the import side (consider, for example, the case of a compliant good – say, a component like a pressure vessel – which is seen by national authorities as not compliant with local law, but only because the country is late or incorrect in implementation of EU rules, and which is needed in the value-chain for producing final goods domestically and/or for exports).

In short, enforcement barriers generate unjustified costs or hindrances or uncertainty for cross-border business and, in so doing, undermine the very purpose of the single market. Besides this direct effect, there are indirect consequences such as a reduction of competitive pressures in the relevant national market, thereby mitigating one of the sources of longer-term economic growth arising from the internal market. For consumers it is possibly harmful, too, since, as long as enforcement failures continue, they might be deprived from benefiting from greater choice between variants of goods and services and/or cheaper offerings from elsewhere in the EU, or, perhaps be exposed to goods or services with a higher risk than agreed by the EU legislature.

The following illustration might clarify this rather general discussion. In the internal market for goods, a very large part of the EU regulatory *acquis* has to do with technical directives or regulations. Enforcement barriers would arise from non-enforcement/non-implementation/bad

---

resulting from the acts of the institutions of the Union". In addition, member states shall facilitate the achievement of the Union's tasks and refrain from any measure that could jeopardise the attainment of the Union's objectives. Also, "the Union and the member states shall…assist each other in carrying out tasks which flow from the Treaties". Art. 291/1, TFEU says that member states "shall adopt all measures of national law necessary to implement legally binding Union acts".

application of EU directives or regulations, but – possibly – also from imposing non-compliant standards (directly or via insurance contracts) and/or from inappropriate testing, certification or even accreditation. However, there is one other possibility that is *not*, strictly speaking, an 'enforcement barrier'. Even when free movement is not at issue in any way and access is not more costly than expected, the internal market may suffer from a *distortion*. In the case of technical regulation, one can think of *market surveillance* which is one of several ways to enforce EU law in a member state. If market surveillance is weak or absent, free movement is not hindered but competitive goods may come into the market that are not 'EU law-compliant' – often, cheaper by virtue of by-passing costly safety or environmental provisions in EU law – and hence imply a competitive disadvantage for EU law-compliant goods. A distortion of this kind is surely due to an enforcement *failure*, yet without in itself raising costs or hindrances in cross-border activities. See Figure 1 for a summary.

Figure 1. Enforcement failures: Barriers and distortions

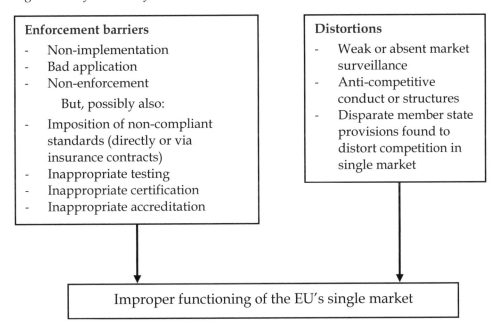

Indeed, the proper functioning of the internal market is not only about (having no 'barriers' to) free movement and establishment, but also about the avoidance of distortions (at least, as far as the EU has competence) such as anti-competitive conduct or structures, or, as in the case at hand, unequal conditions caused by a failure to apply EU law improperly. This study does not deal with *market surveillance* by the member states, since it is strictly speaking not a barrier.[5]

The right-hand box in Figure 1 also refers to distortive disparities of national regulation or administrative handling as mentioned in Arts 116 and 117, TFEU. Thus, if regulatory heterogeneity between member states using their regulatory autonomy is regarded by the Commission as "distorting competition in the internal market", the EU legislature can intervene with a conciliation procedure or, as a fallback power, a directive eliminating the distortion. These articles are rarely used for reasons of subsidiarity (not too easily overruling national regulatory autonomy) and the difficulty of operationalising the generic economic term 'distortion'. In other words, there is large discretion for regulatory heterogeneity generated by member states and only a residual EU competence to intervene in extreme cases. Except in special cases, European business will have to live with (minor, yet irritating) distortions as a result of lingering regulatory heterogeneity in the single market.

---

[5] Depending on the sector, consumers and/or businesses have called attention to the inadequacies of national market surveillance. Examples include toys, pressure equipment, cosmetic products and motor vehicles (which are even 'type-approval' in principle). Under the market surveillance Regulation No. (EC) 765/2008, member states must allocate 'sufficient resources' to market surveillance. According to Orgalime, the European Engineering Industries Association, this is far from being the case. For more information, see http://ec.europa.eu/ enterprise/sectors/mechanical/machinery/market-surveillance/index_en.htm

3. TYPOLOGY OF EU ENFORCEMENT BARRIERS

In this chapter, we ask the question whether a typology of enforcement barriers can be developed, before we go on to survey the entire landscape of EU enforcement in chapter 4, and its elaboration, step by step, in the subsequent chapters. The use of a typology may be found in a more aggregated view of the problem than an elaborate panoramic perspective, which we hope to offer in this study. In other words, it might be helpful for EU and national policy-makers as well as economists interested in attempting to calculate estimates per type (given the different properties of each type and the derived effects in markets).

Nevertheless, as this study will once again confirm, enforcement in the EU internal market is a complicated domain, with considerable sophistication and much institutional and legal subtlety. It is also, by definition, a profound issue of the EU's two-level government system. These fundamentals render this area quite resistant to generalisations, which are a prerequisite for any typology to be useful. 'The' EU internal market consists of five distinct market types: goods, services, labour, capital and codified technology (like patents). It is problematic to transfer a typology developed for goods markets to any one of the other four markets, or, indeed, the other way around. The present study is mostly focused on goods. Barriers in e.g. the internal market for services, and the enforcement barriers as a sequel, are both quite different and considerably harder to classify, and possibly more numerous as well.[6] But even in goods, the variety of remaining barriers in the EU internal market is still large and enforcement of EU rules and principles is far from simple or uniform.

---

[6] See for example the well-known Commission survey, "The state of the internal market for services", COM(2002) 441 of 30 July 2002, where no less than 90 (!) types of barriers were identified. The reader is also referred to Mustilli & Pelkmans (2012) on the identification of barriers in the EU internal market for services, in the framework of the FP7 project SERVICEGAP.

Later in this study, we shall provide detailed empirical evidence on (enforcement) barriers or failures, drawing on several sources. First, we report on the on-line problem-solving network called SOLVIT.[7] Secondly, we provide a comprehensive assessment of member states' notifications under Directive 98/34 (on any technical regulation at national level, published in summary form on the TRIS website,[8] maintained by DG Enterprise and Industry of the European Commission. And finally, we explore recent case law where relevant trends in CJEU infringement cases, preceded by the Commission's efforts to realise compliance without going to the CJEU. We shall demonstrate that these efforts to overcome or remove 'enforcement barriers' are quite different in nature (e.g. some are 'preventive', other ex-post). It may well be possible to derive a useful typology from all these enforcement efforts in the landscape to be sketched.

We will confine our discussion to a simple typology, mainly as an introduction to the reader and a warning about a few suggestions sometimes made in the EU debates.

Enforcement barriers could best be regarded as barriers to (intra-EU) market access that have not been addressed effectively by EU enforcement mechanisms although they should have been. Therefore, enforcement barriers are a direct consequence of the *acquis communautaire*, hence, what has already been accomplished in the EU internal market. Enforcement barriers exclude lingering barriers that are the result of a failure at EU level to harmonise or a lack of Commission initiatives to this effect, or derogations in the treaty about a few remaining areas of national regulatory competences (which leave member states 'free' to act on their own). For European business or consumers, such fine distinctions will often be far removed from their concerns: usually, for them, these instances are barriers, no matter what labels are attached to them.

---

[7] Created in July 2002, the SOLVIT network allows EU member states to work together to solve problems caused by the misapplication of internal market law by public authorities without taking recourse to legal proceedings. SOLVIT centres handle complaints from both citizens and businesses. Each EU member state (as well as Norway, Iceland and Liechtenstein) has its own SOLVIT centre. Their services are free of charge and aim to solve problems within ten weeks. For more information, see the SOLVIT website of the European Commission, which coordinates the network (http://ec.europa.eu/solvit/site/index_en.htm).

[8] TRIS stands for Technical Regulations Information Systems. For more information, see http://ec.europa.eu/enterprise/tris/index_en.htm

In terms of public actors, it might be useful to distinguish 'legislative' enforcement barriers (in which the legislator in each member state is to be addressed) from 'administrative' barriers. In the latter, the national law itself is not the problem, but rather it is the practical, administrative execution (and the agencies, bodies or administrative units in the national governments) that is in need of correction or discipline. Legislative barriers include late or incorrect transposition of EU directives, national technical requirements in laws and decrees causing barriers (despite mutual recognition) and the question of national gold-plating of EU directives. Insofar as business is internationalised in European if not world-wide value-chains, the goods markets may also be affected (negatively) by higher costs originating from (too) restrictive service regulation, since these are usually closely connected inside value-chains. The so-called 'knock-on' effects of restrictive service regulation for manufacturing industries and their trade can be quite high.[9] They can surely be regarded as barriers, and hence bad enforcement in the internal market for services also hinders the proper functioning of the internal goods market.

Administrative barriers include the incorrect application of EU directives, conformity assessment barriers and enforcement issues in (intra-EU) public procurement, especially non-publication (when above the value thresholds in EU law).

Gold-plating

Our study goes at length into the first two instances of legislative barriers. The following two barriers call for a comment, however. First, what exactly is 'gold-plating' and when is it a barrier? The practical problem of gold-plating is that it is a much-used term in the EU circuit, but very little rigorous analysis has been undertaken. The broad idea is that member states 'use' the occasion of the duty to implement a directive in such a way that either other or additional requirements (preferred in that country but not harmonised in Brussels) are added in the national law, or that the transposition is combined with revisions of related legislation that have

---

[9] See Conway & Nicoletti (2006, Figure 23) for this 'knock-on' effect for EU15 countries and some other OECD countries in 2003 (ranging from a factor of 0.1 up to 0.35) and Arnold et al. (2011, p. 104) for the knock-on effect on ICT-using and non-ICT-using sectors in 2003 (ranging from 0.08 to 0.27 for ICT-using sectors). The latter distinction is motivated by the growth restraints caused by knock-on effects, shown to have been most damaging in the ICT-using sectors.

nothing to do with the directive at stake (but one cannot 'see' that from the text). Gold-plating has received a bad name because extra national requirements or too stringent formulations, not necessary for the directive to be implemented, are – more often than not – associated in business circles, the press or in populist political parties with 'Brussels', portrayed as "again" adding to the regulatory burden or imposing "silly" demands. It is exceedingly hard to find out, case by case in each member state, whether these extras are due to the EU decisions (with the relevant country explicitly involved, by the way), to the member state itself when implementing the regulation or to the member state itself but for reasons beyond the scope of EU competences.

Therefore, one has to be careful in equating gold-plating with enforcement barriers. One can safely associate gold-plating with problems of market access for business from other member states (and most likely for local business as well), but is it an enforcement failure or barrier? A priori, one cannot tell because the 'extra' provisions 'around' the requirements of the relevant directive may well be legitimate and legal under national regulatory autonomy. Thus, whilst it may increase 'regulatory heterogeneity' (and this might be costly for business),[10] there is no lack of enforcement.

So, gold-plating necessitates a careful study of each and every case, and, in many instances, enforcement might not be the issue. The only authoritative study on gold-plating, the UK Davidson Review (Davidson, 2006, p. 4), expresses a similar view:

> The review found that properly assessing whether a particular piece of European legislation has in fact been over-implemented and whether that over-implementation is justified is not straightforward. The assessment requires careful research into the legislation and the policy reasons behind the UK's implementation, as well as consideration of how the legislation is being enforced in practice and the impacts it has on those being regulated.

It is also interesting to examine how gold-plating is defined. The Review's wording is: "when implementation goes beyond the minimum necessary to comply" in four ways: extending the scope, not taking full advantage of derogations, employing sanctions or e.g. the burden of proof

---

[10] See the seminal works by Kox & Lejour (2006) with respect to the Services Directive, and Nordås & Kox (2009) for an extension with respect to the costs of heterogeneity. These costs can be quite high.

beyond the minimum needed or too early implementation (Davidson, 2006, p. 5). Note that the last one is dubious, to say the least, and even the second one is problematic, since it assumes that EU law is somehow (too?) costly and is not a better arrangement for market functioning. Indeed, in some cases, derogations might be distortive (but were accepted as the price of compromise in EU decision-making between 27 countries), and they almost always cause more heterogeneity.

Technical requirements

The 'barrier' of technical requirements also calls for a precise statement. Recently, the EU regime for mutual recognition (until that moment, based on CJEU case law) has decisively changed with Regulation 764/2008.[11] First, in principle, member states *must* have a single contact point for free information for business and reference to the competent authorities on any such laws (thus, spending resources should now be minimised). Second, if mutual recognition is incorrectly applied, the burden-of-proof is now on the member state, with considerable protection of the company wanting market access for its good. The expected effect of this reversal is that incorrect application of mutual recognition has been made rather difficult. Third, if technical requirements are justified, e.g. by health reasons, one should normally expect it to be under EU regulation already. If not, it would fall in a relatively limited category of (yet) unresolved lingering barriers to intra-EU market access, which can be costly, but it does *not* constitute an enforcement barrier (because EU law does not yet apply).

Under administrative barriers, we shall treat the first one at length in the rest of the study. The second one (under the label 'conformity assessment') might here and there still exist, but one should take into account that the 2008 so-called 'New Legislative Framework' has addressed these barriers very carefully indeed with Regulation EC/765/2008 and Decision 768/2008, and their subsequent application to the 2009 revised toy Directive as well as nine other new approach directives.[12]

---

[11] Regulation EC/764/2008 of 9 July 2008 laying down procedures relating to the application of certain technical rules to products lawfully marketed in another member state, OJEC L 218 of 13 August 2008.

[12] Reg. 765/2008 of 9 July 2008 setting out the requirements for accreditation and market surveillance relating to the marketing of products, OJEC L 218 of 13 August 2008; Decision 768/2008 on a common framework for the marketing of products, OJEC L 218 of 13 August 2008.

4. THE LANDSCAPE OF EU ENFORCEMENT EFFORTS

Not only has the EU strict treaty articles on the member states' duties of enforcement, the machinery to realise such enforcement and to correct bad (national) enforcement has expanded considerably over time. The time has long passed when enforcement was the exclusive domain of lawyers, even if the ultimate 'hard core' powers of the EU consist of recourse to the CJEU (with fines, in extreme instances). Figure 2 shows the entire landscape of enforcement of single market law. Three of the five types of enforcement efforts have been available since the outset of the European Economic Community (EEC): detection (via monitoring and complaints), pre-infringement initiatives and formal infringement procedures. As we shall see in the following sections, however, the scope of efforts in the former two has widened appreciably over time.

Figure 2. Enforcement of single market law

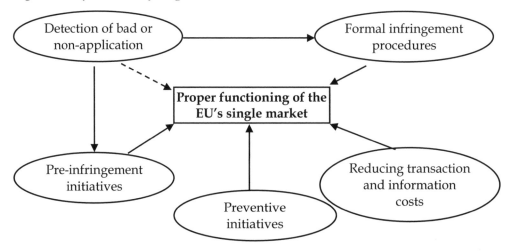

More recently, emphasis has been given to effective prevention in a number of ways. Lowering the transaction and information costs of business (and sometimes consumers) associated with perceived or actual 'barriers' to intra-EU market access has also become far more important. These two types of efforts are not always clearly distinct – there can be some overlap for a few activities. The overall conclusion suggested strongly by Figure 2 is that complaints about insufficient or ineffective enforcement have been around for decades and that the EU level as well as member states have responded (with some delays, to be sure) with more, and more differentiated, efforts. The reader will notice in the following sections that especially the *preventive* measures have expanded enormously, closely followed by much greater intensity of *pre-infringement* efforts, with the aim of pre-empting enforcement barriers or nipping them in the bud at low costs when detected.

Detection of incorrect implementation (transposition) and/or bad enforcement of single market law in the member states used to be the exclusive activity of the European Commission, surrounded by confidentiality on the EU/member states' interface. This was a consequence of the original emphasis on formal infringement efforts as spelled out in the treaty. Of course, even in the formal approach, the treaty encourages (after detection) informal interaction between the Commission and the member states with a view to resolving the problem immediately without further proceedings. As Figure 14 shows (Chapter 6), no less than 70% of detections are solved this way! Nowadays, however, detection and pre-infringement efforts have become ever more closely related and the initial secrecy has largely disappeared. The idea behind that is probably that timely and effective detection is in the common interest of all economic agents in the single market. Indeed, detection is, more often than not, the result of private agents encountering doubtful or plainly illegal provisions or hindrances, so that public encouragement of filing complaints and regular publicity as well as accessible mechanisms to report are raising the effectiveness of enforcement. Thus, the Petitions Committee of the European Parliament may bring up cases reported to them and some of the pre-infringement mechanisms (such as SOLVIT, package meetings, networks of officials, scoreboards – see chapter 5) may also be supportive of the detection function.

5. PRE-INFRINGEMENT INITIATIVES

The actual implementation of internal market law is still facing major challenges, such as considerable delays in transposing directives into national law[13] or an increased number of complaints from citizens and enterprises concerning the violation of their rights granted by EU law.

The European Commission, as 'guardian of the treaties', shall oversee the application of EU law under the control of the CJEU (Art. 17 (1) TFEU). In carrying out this mission and given slow legal procedures, the Commission continuously developed new ways to enhance the implementation and enforcement of EU law. Of course, the classical legal enforcement in the treaty remains the hard-core instrument in the EU. However, much effort during recent decades has been invested in working around it or finding complementary ways of realising greater effectiveness. This is good policy because the drawbacks of formal infringement procedures are considerable. And, even more important, it does not result in a degree of effectiveness that European business (or, indeed, customers and consumers!) nowadays is impressed by. One must keep this method and the powers at Commission/CJEU level as a hard fall-back option, but much more is necessary if one wants the single market to function

---

[13] See Internal Market Scoreboard No. 23, of September 2011. It shows that, for the first time since 2007, member states have exceeded the 1% transposition deficit (note that this 1% target is a reduction from the earlier 1½% target). For the notifications of directives with a transposition deadline of 30 April 2011, notified by 10 May 2011, the average transposition deficit was 1.2%. The percentage of incorrectly transposed directives in July 2011 was 0.8%, which is above the 0.5% target recently proposed in the Single Market Act of 13 April 2011. For the latter, see Commission Communication, "Single Market Act: Twelve levers to boost growth and strengthen confidence – 'Working together to create new growth'", COM (2011) 206, 14 April 2011.

properly. Much greater emphasis has been given to a range of pre-infringement initiatives, that is, once a complaint arises and is picked up by the Commission (as the guardian of the treaties), there are many ways to arrive at a solution before one ends up in Luxembourg at the CJEU.

The pre-infringement landscape is wide, ranging from the informal and formal steps of the earlier stages of the infringement procedure (discussed as part of infringement procedures, see chapter 6), to so-called 'package meetings' with member states, to setting up specialised networks of national civil servants dealing with specific EU legislation helping with interpretation issues of complex directives (e.g. the machine Directive or type-approval questions or of national banking supervision exceptions to EU rules). A new variant of these pre-infringement efforts consists of several informal approaches, which help to reduce the lack of compliance by member states, such as the SOLVIT network, but also the regular publication of the Internal Market Scoreboard with records of each member state in (late) implementation of EU legislation, which, in turn, creates Commission and inter-member state peer pressures to improve the scores.[14] Of these many efforts, we shall elaborate on the SOLVIT network, the European Consumer Centres Network (ECC-Net) and two Scoreboards (one on the internal market and one on consumer issues) in chapters 5 and 6 (sections 5.1, 5.2 and 6.2.1.2).

These 'soft' and flexible instruments, providing a less intrusive and often not so legalistic way to ensure the observance of EU legislation, have a practical influence transcending their informal character. Moreover, the *member states* have become central to greater effectiveness in this respect. Hence, both the pre-infringement and the preventive approaches rely more and more, although not exclusively, on the active *cooperation* of member states, as a group, or between the member states and the Commission, in sharp contrast to formal infringement procedures where "the" EU (via the Commission) *opposes* a member state in a legal proceeding.

---

[14] Note that these pressures are augmented by CJEU case law making an EU country liable, with possible damages to be paid to e.g. business, in national lawsuits for non-implementation.

5.1 The SOLVIT network

5.1.1 Background and functioning of the SOLVIT network

One of the ways in which the Commission has tried to solve problems that arise for citizens and businesses from the misapplication of internal market law is the creation of SOLVIT.

Set up in 2002, by European Commission Communication on Effective Problem Solving in the Internal Market (SOLVIT),[15] SOLVIT is an online network for settling cross-border disputes informally over the incorrect and inaccurate application of the single market rules arising between citizens or businesses and public administrations across EU member states, to the extent that such disputes are not subject to legal proceedings at national or EU level. SOLVIT is meant as an informal alternative to other problem-solving mechanisms, such as national court procedures, formal complaints to the European Commission and petitions.

The system is based on mutual cooperation[16] and online techniques that allow for a decisional procedure, which are easily accessible, free of charge, and offer a quick solution to the internal market problems.

---

[15] In fact, an earlier version of SOLVIT had existed since 1997, following the Commission Communication Action Plan for the Single Market, in accordance with the 1996 Council Resolution on cooperation between administrations for the enforcement of legislation on the internal market. However, this problem-solving network did not work effectively and in 2001, the Commission proposed a newer version, effective as of 2002. The new system is based on the pre-existing cooperation network, on an online database connecting the centres and principles for centres to follow when dealing with the cases (which are set out in the Recommendation of the Commission on principles for using SOLVIT – the Internal Market Problem Solving Network). See Communication from the Commission to the Council, the European Parliament, the Economic and Social Committee and the Committee of the Regions – "Effective Problem Solving in the Internal Market (SOLVIT)", COM(2001)702 final; European Commission Recommendation of 7 December 2001 on principles for using SOLVIT – The Internal Market Problem Solving Network, OJ L 33; European Commission Communication "Action Plan for the single market", of 4 June 1997, CSE (97) I final and Council Resolution of 8 July 1996 on "Cooperation between administrations for the enforcement of legislation on the internal market", 96/C 224/02.

[16] The system is drawn up on the principle of mutual cooperation at three different levels: at cross-border level between the two centres involved in the decision procedure (the so-called 'home' centre and the 'lead' centre); at national level

There is a national SOLVIT centre in every EU member state as well as Iceland, Liechtenstein and Norway, which is part of the member states' national administration (most centres are either based in the Ministry of Foreign Affairs or the Ministry of Economic Affairs) and is subject to the law of the member states. SOLVIT centres cooperate directly with each other via an online database. The Commission is generally not directly involved in this alternative informal dispute settlement system. However, the Commission coordinates the network; provides, manages and controls the database (which connects the national SOLVIT Centres); and, when needed, helps speed up the resolution of problems. The Commission is also responsible for ensuring that "all proposed solutions should be in full conformity with Community law".[17] In 2004, the Commission published a Staff Working Document aimed at setting out in operational terms the approach to exercise its activity.[18] DG Internal Market should organise periodic evaluations of the SOLVIT network including the range of solutions implemented, in particular to address evident problems. Moreover, the Commission always retains its prerogative to start an infringement proceeding, under Art. 258 TFEU, whenever this is necessary.

At same time, SOLVIT is an online alternative dispute resolution mechanism (ODR)[19] and a cooperation network between national administrations, which contributes to improving the implementation capacity of EU law at national level and hence fosters the correct application of EU law. In fact, evaluation shows that SOLVIT centres contribute to a "cultural change" in their own national civil service.[20]

(between the lead centre and the national administration, which allegedly acted in breach of EU law) and at European level (between the centres and the European Commission).

[17] European Commission Recommendation on "Principles for using SOLVIT – the Internal Market Problem Solving Network", C(2001)390, 7 December 2001.

[18] See European Commission Staff Working Document "Setting out the approach for assessing the conformity of solutions proposed by SOLVIT network with Community Law", (2004), 17 September 2004, SEC(2004)1159.

[19] In contrast to the infringement procedures as defined under Arts 258 and 260 TFEU, SOLVIT is an alternative, complementary out-of-court dispute settlement mechanism.

[20] See European Commission Evaluation of SOLVIT, Final Report, November 2011.

Today, SOLVIT handles around 1,300 cases a year (in 2011, SOLVIT received a total of 3,154 cases, of which 1,306 fell within its mandate) and manages to find solutions for over 89% of its clients, with an average turnaround time of 70 days.[21]

In practice, SOLVIT works as follows. When a citizen or a business has a complaint concerning the application of internal market rules by the public authorities of another member state, he can lodge this complaint at the SOLVIT centre in his own country (the so-called 'home' centre).[22] SOLVIT centres in principle only act following the initiative of a citizen or business confronted with a problem, but they can also take the initiative of identifying and contacting citizens or businesses directly to solve their problem. According to the European Commission, these initiatives should be encouraged and SOLVIT centres should be able to mark their 'own initiative' cases as such in the SOLVIT database.[23] It is also possible that the Commission relays a complaint it has received through other channels to the SOLVIT centre, if it believes the problem could be solved in a satisfactory manner without its own involvement. Out of the 4,035 cases entered into CHAP (the Commission's complaints handling system) in 2010, 22 cases were referred on to SOLVIT.[24]

The home centre, after receiving the complaint, has to make a preliminary assessment in order to verify whether the case falls under the scope of the SOLVIT system or whether it could be better resolved by other means or legal proceedings would be more appropriate. It has to verify whether the problem has a cross-border dimension, involves the application of internal market rules and is concerned with a dispute between a citizen or business and a national public administration.[25]

---

[21] See European Commission, "Making the Single Market deliver, Annual governance check-up 2011", 2012.

[22] The applicant does not need to meet any particular requirements and the case can be submitted to his home centre in his own language.

[23] European Commission, DG Internal Market and Services, Working Paper, "Reinforcing effective problem-solving in the Single Market: Unlocking SOLVIT's full potential at the occasion of its 10th anniversary", 2012.

[24] Ibid.

[25] The SOLVIT system offers help in cases concerning problems of a cross-border nature involving a public authority, but not B2B (business to business) or B2C

It should be noted that one of the main problems faced by the SOLVIT system since its creation is the number of cases landing on SOLVIT's desk that fall outside its mandate. In response to submissions outside its remit, SOLVIT centres either helped to solve the problem informally, explored other problem-solving possibilities or pointed citizens and businesses in the right direction. A positive development in 2011 was precisely the lower percentage of cases referred to SOLVIT that fell outside its remit (see Figure 3 below).[26]

Figure 3. Total number of cases submitted to SOLVIT and to the 'Your Europe Advice' (YEA) portal, 2003-11

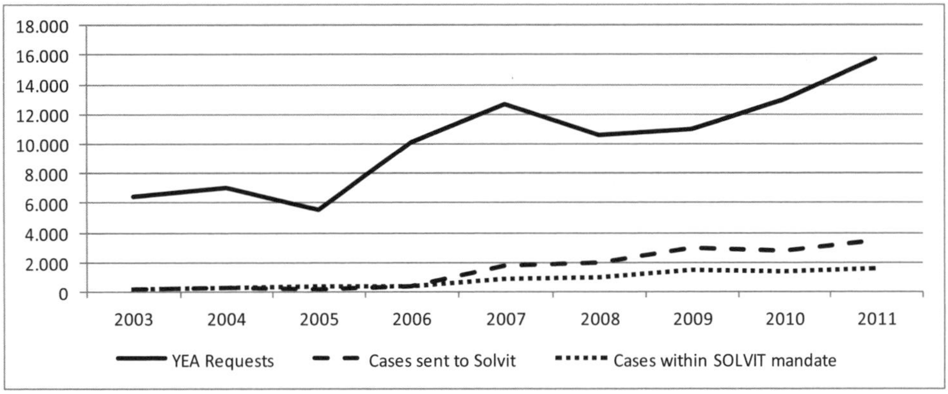

Source: Redrawn from European Commission, "Making the Single Market deliver: Annual governance check-up 2011", Brussels, 2011, p. 25.

If the claim is found to be well founded and is not already the subject of a legal proceeding,[27] the home centre forwards the case to the centre of

---

(business to consumer) disputes or disputes where judicial procedures are already underway.

[26] This development is probably linked to the rise in requests dealt with by the 'Your Europe Advice' (YEA) portal, an EU advice service for the public, currently provided by legal experts from the European Citizen Action Service (ECAS) operating under contract with the European Commission. It consists of a team of lawyers who cover all EU official languages and are familiar both with EU law and national laws in all EU countries. YEA cooperates closely with SOLVIT and a common online form directs questions to most appropriate service.

[27] In accordance with the 2001 Recommendation on the principles for using SOLVIT, the home centre cannot enter the case in the database if it is already the

the member state in which the cross-border problem occurred (the so-called 'lead' centre) by entering it into the database and making all the relevant information available. The lead centre verifies whether there has been a breach of the EU law. If the case is accepted[28] (deadline: one week), the two SOLVIT centres will work together in solving the problem within a target deadline of 10 weeks. Given this short deadline, the SOLVIT centres are allowed to refuse cases that require a change in national law or other implementing provisions (the so-called 'SOLVIT-Plus' cases),[29] since these would be too difficult to handle via informal means within 10 weeks. However, many centres accept some of these cases and are able to offer more structural solutions and not only solve the individual case at hand.

Within this period of time, the lead centre will seek the necessary evidence and legal advice to solve the case, contact the public administration that allegedly violated the single market legislation and try to negotiate a proposed solution to the problem with the public authority. The proposed solution by the lead centre is not binding on the administration (or the complainant). The final decision is taken by the national administration. When a solution is found, the lead and the home centres should confirm their agreement and inform the complainant. Furthermore, the complainant does not have to accept the proposed solution. However, the final solution can only be challenged by the complainant through a more time-consuming legal action.[30]

5.1.2 *Performance of the SOLVIT Network in 2011*

During the SOLVIT network's first eight years of existence (2003-09), the volume of cases rose continuously. Beginning with less than 200 (2003), 300 (2004), 400 (2005-06) leading up to more than 1,000 cases in 2008 and with 1,540 cases reported in 2009. After 2009, the number of cases remained stable with only a few fluctuations (Figure 3).

---

subject of legal proceedings. Moreover, if an applicant decides, at any stage, to initiate legal proceedings, the case should be removed from the database.

[28] If the lead centre dismisses the case, it has to indicate the reasons for the rejection.

[29] SOLVIT Plus cases are discussed in section 5.1.5.

[30] Commission Staff Working Document, "Setting out the approach for assessing the conformity of solutions proposed by SOLVIT network with Community law", SEC (2004) 1159, Brussels 17 September 2004.

In 2011, SOLVIT handled a total of 3,154 cases, of which 1,306 fell within its mandate. Compared with 2010, the total number of cases submitted to SOLVIT was slightly lower (in 2010, SOLVIT handled 3,800 cases, of which 1,363 fell within its competence).[31]

One of the biggest problems with the SOLVIT system since it was set up is the amount of cases submitted to the centres that are outside their competence. The overwhelming majority of such cases concern requests for information and advice. SOLVIT usually directs these cases to more relevant sources of help, e.g. 'Your Europe Advice (YEA), EURES (European Enterprise Network) and the European Consumer Centres. However, it is undeniable that the large number of non-SOLVIT cases dealt with by the network is an obstacle to its effectiveness, especially since centres generally remain understaffed. Indeed, this adds significantly to SOLVIT's workload, since all of these cases need to be examined in order to determine whether they should be handled by SOLVIT, and, if not, they are then forwarded to a more appropriate address. In order to solve this problem, the Commission, in 2008, published an Action Plan to help citizens and businesses better understand and make use of their rights in the EU,[32] containing a plan for streamlining a whole range of existing information and assistance services, including SOLVIT, which should bring about better filtering of cases at the point of entry. The action plan includes the setting up of a 'single contact point', where citizens will be referred to the entity that may best serve them.

As a result of the Single Market Assistance Services (SMAS), action plan, the Commission has completely revamped the 'Your Europe' portal and is committed to further developing and promoting it. The new 'Your Europe' offers user-friendly information about EU rights and helps people find further advice and help when needed. Moreover, via intelligent on-online forms, 'Your Europe' immediately refers people asking for more advice or help to the right service. Despite or because of these improvements, the number of visits to the 'Your Europe' website is growing exponentially. In addition, it appears that SOLVIT centres are

---

[31] The drop in the number of cases can be attributed to the decrease of certain types of residence cases in the UK, which had produced a large number of similar complaints in 2009-10.

[32] See Commission Staff Working Paper, "Action plan on an integrated approach for providing Single Market Assistance Services to citizens and businesses", SEC(2008)188, of 8 May 2008.

receiving fewer requests for information and advice, which might well be due to a more effective common intake form. Furthermore, Europe Direct is also further developing its capacity to filter requests, so that they reach the right service, and to facilitate an easy transfer between the systems. On the other hand, the filter system should also lead to an increase in cases where SOLVIT can provide real help, but where citizens and businesses currently have difficulties finding their way to SOLVIT. A positive development in 2011 was precisely the reduced percentage of cases referred to SOLVIT that fell outside its remit (Figure 3).

The levels of resolution rates remained high and stable at 89% (compared to 90% in 2010) (see Figure 4).

Figure 4. Resolution rates of the SOLVIT cases during SOLVIT's mandate, 2003-11

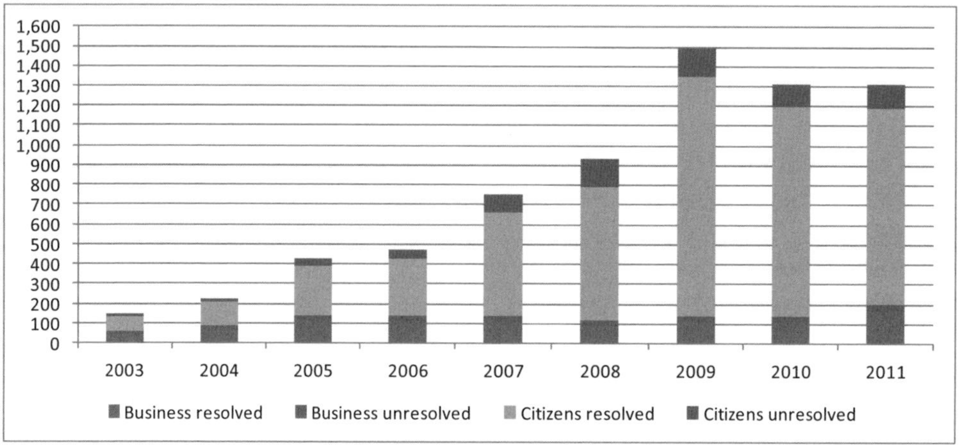

Source: Redrawn from European Commission, "Making the Single Market deliver: Annual governance check-up 2011", 2011, p. 26.

It should be noted that resolved cases often not only solve the problems encountered by an individual citizen or business, but also generate changes in attitude, work practices or legal rules that benefit a larger number of people who would otherwise have encountered the same problem.[33] On the other hand, unresolved cases are 'useful' as well, since

---

[33] This could be illustrated by a large number of cases dealt with SOLVIT Ireland in the social security area. As result of its involvement, the competent Irish authorities have put in place procedures to allow for a more efficient handling of social security complaints and thus removed the backlog that had existed. As a

they point to particular problems that need to be addressed to improve the functioning of the single market.[34]

The member states that submitted and received the largest number of cases in 2011 are France, Spain, Germany and Italy. In 2011 we observe an increase in the number of cases submitted and received in Germany, Austria, France, Denmark and Luxembourg. The number of cases received by Ireland decreased substantially due to the reduction of social security cases, since the underlying problem was resolved by the Irish authorities (see Figure 5 below).

Figure 5. Number of cases submitted to and received by the national SOLVIT centres, 2010-11

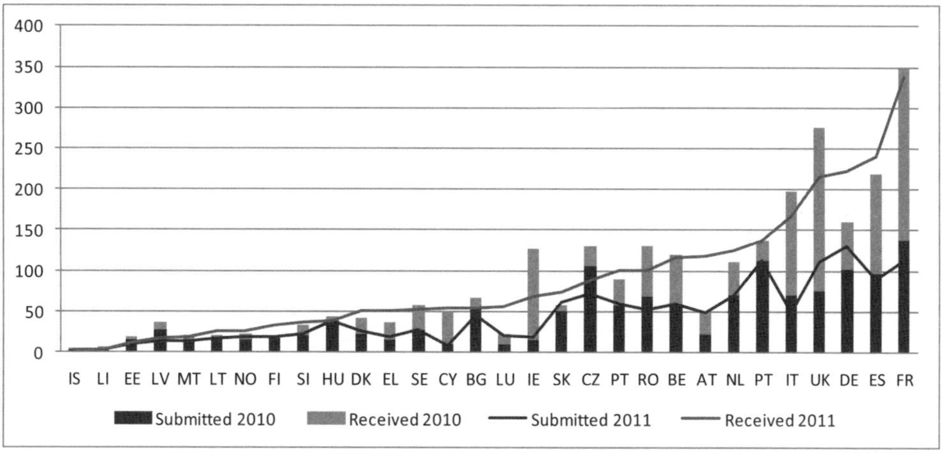

Source: Redrawn from European Commission, "Making the Single Market deliver: Annual governance check-up 2011", 2011, p. 27.

---

consequence, the number of complaints in this area dropped significantly. Another example occurred in Portugal, where following the intervention of SOLVIT Portugal, a local authority no longer requires a medical assistance card for British citizens residing in Portugal to be renewed on an annual basis, an administrative practice that was not in line with EU law.

[34] An example is found in the large number of cases concerning VAT reimbursement in Luxembourg, because of the introduction of an electronic reimbursement system. The unresolved cases were brought to the ministers' attention and were subsequently addressed. The same happened with the unresolved cases concerning the recognition of the professional qualifications of Romanian nurses in Spain.

SOLVIT intervention is particularly significant in specific areas of the internal market, where quick and/or cost-effective solutions are needed. In 2011, as in 2010, social security issues related to migrants generated the largest number of cases (39% in 2011, 34% in 2010). The proportion of cases concerning the recognition of professional qualifications remained at around 15%. The number of cases concerning residence permits decreased to 12% (from 23% in 2010).[35] Problems also occurred in relation to the free movement of services and goods, taxation and motor vehicles registration and driving licenses. Cases involving the free movement of goods and services remained at 8%, while the number of taxation cases increased from 5% to 9% in relation to the last period (see Figure 6 below).

Figure 6. 2011 SOLVIT cases by area

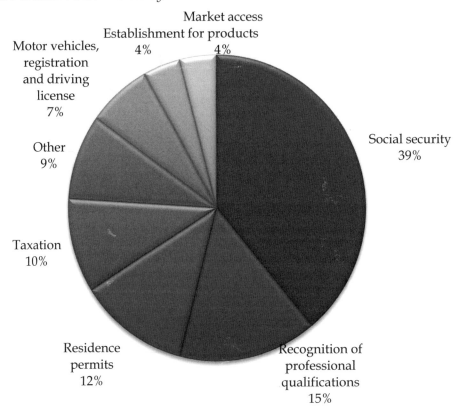

----

[35] This is mainly because the number of residence permit cases received by the UK SOLVIT centre fell from 419 in 2009, to 185 in 2010 and 37 in 2011.

A closer look at the cases handled by SOLVIT in the area of social security shows that the vast majority of them involve cross-border problems related to recognition of basic pension rights acquired in other EU countries, payment of family allowances, coverage of medical treatment and payment of other social benefits.

One of the main challenges to the SOLVIT network is how to enhance its capacity for dealing with social security cases, by strengthening synergies between SOLVIT and the Administrative Commission for the Coordination of the Social Security Schemes.[36] The Administrative Commission for the Coordination of Social Security Schemes (Admin Comm) is a specialised body composed of social security experts within national administrations. Its objective is to clarify EU regulations and administrative practices relating to social security issues as well as clarify questions of interpretation.[37] The Administrative Commission only deals with complaints received via the Commission, but citizens, workers and business can contact SOLVIT centres directly when they face cross-border problems related to social security issues. Experience has shown that, in some cases, the SOLVIT centres don't have the necessary legal expertise to deal with such cases, in particular given the fact that, in the area of social security, EU law only coordinates (not harmonises) national rules. Moreover, when SOLVIT centres ask for legal advice from the Administrative Commission, it frequently fails to meet SOLVIT deadlines due to the complexity of the cases and the fact that its timeframes are less strict than those of SOLVIT. On the other hand, individuals of the Administrative Commission often receive complaints about cross-border problems related to the application of social security rules, but they do not have effective tools for dealing with such complaints. Therefore, increasing the synergies and the cooperation between SOLVIT and the Administrative Commission in the future will help to achieve more effective results when handling social security complaints. The European Commission plans to send the complaints in the area of social security to SOLVIT and, at same time, ensure that SOLVIT can rely more systematically on legal advice from the Administrative Commission.

---

[36] Regulation (EC) No 883/2004, of 29 April 2004, on the coordination of the social security system.

[37] The Administrative Commission also supports coordination of social security schemes, promotes dialogue, reconciliation and the exchange of best practices, collects statistics and reviews coordination provisions.

Recognition of professional qualifications[38] is one of the other main areas in which SOLVIT cases occurred. In the period 2010-11, a total of 408 opened and closed cases were registered in this field, of which 53 were unresolved and 355 were resolved. These cases include the unjustified refusal to recognise certain qualifications, the failure to offer the possibility to compensate for differences in qualifications and the passing of legal deadlines for processing requests for recognition.

Various SOLVIT cases involved the correct application of Art. 34 TFEU on the free movement of goods and of the mutual recognition principle, by facilitating market access of products legally produced or sold in other EU member states.

At times, intervention by the SOLVIT centres has exceeded the ambit outlined in the SOLVIT background documents.[39] SOLVIT is aimed at resolving individual cross-border problems caused by decisional obstacles due to a public administration's incorrect application of European internal market rules, when, because of the particular nature of the situation, the recourse to a national court would (or could) be ineffective, take too long or be too expensive. This means, firstly, that SOLVIT's scope is limited to the problems encountered by citizens and business related to the application of internal market rules. Secondly, SOLVIT's centres should only handle cases

---

[38] On 19 December 2011, the European Commission presented a proposal for a revision of Directive 2005/36/EC on the recognition of professional qualifications. The objective of the proposal is to facilitate the speedy recognition of professional qualifications to support the mobility of professionals across the single market. To this end, the Commission has proposed the introduction of an electronic European Professional Card, which will be implemented through the existing Internal Market Information system (IMI). An alert mechanism to identify health professionals guilty of malpractice is also proposed. The proposal will modernise the harmonised minimum training requirements for certain professions benefiting from automatic recognition (in particular doctors, nurses, midwives and architects). It will also offer the possibility to extend automatic recognition to new professions through the concepts of 'common training framework' and 'common training test'. Furthermore, it will simplify access to information on recognition of qualifications by extending the scope of the Points of Single Contact introduced by the Services Directive. For more details, see http://ec.europa.eu/internal_market/ qualifications/policy_developments/index_en.htm

[39] Recommendation on principles for using SOLVIT – The Internal Market Problem-Solving Network and Communication from the Commission, Effective Problem-Solving in the Internal Market (SOLVIT).

where breaches of EU law are caused by a public authority, not by a private party.[40] Thirdly, SOLVIT only deals with cross-border problems; pure domestic problems are excluded from its scope of operation. SOLVIT centres have to dismiss cases that do not fit this description, and, in particular, they should not deal with cases where the individual problems are ultimately caused by a national regulatory barrier.

In practice, however, SOLVIT's mandate has given rise to differences in interpretation and led to different approaches among the national SOLVIT centres when it comes to deciding whether a case should be taken up by SOLVIT or not.[41] Aware of this problem and in order to ensure a coherent approach through the European Union, the Commission, in its document on "Reinforcing effective problem-solving in the internal market",[42] has stressed the necessity to clarify SOLVIT's mandate. Moreover, the Commission considers that, at present, there is no need to further extend SOLVIT's scope. Rather, the focus should be on ensuring that all cases falling within SOLVIT's mandate reach SOLVIT effectively.

As mentioned above, once the case is introduced to the SOLVIT database and accepted by the lead centre, the latter has to try to find a solution for the case within the SOLVIT deadline of ten weeks. In 2011, 67% of the cases were solved within this deadline. However, the average case-handling time was 70 days, four days more than in 2010. Some countries managed to improve their performance (e.g. the UK and Poland), but Austria took significantly more time to handle cases.[43]

---

[40] The Commission services consider that the concept of public authority should be interpreted broadly in order to cover all levels of public administration (national, regional and local authorities) as well as competent authorities (e.g. professional organisations in charge of recognising professional qualifications) and bodies controlled by the state (e.g. universities).

[41] To be more specific, SOLVIT centres have decided cases even when the situation was not 'cross-border' or cases where the entity that allegedly acted in breach of EU law could not be considered a 'public authority' in accordance with national legislation.

[42] See European Commission Working Document, DG Internal Market and Services, "Reinforcing effective problem-solving in the Single Market: Unlocking SOLVIT's full potential on the occasion of its 10th anniversary", 2012.

[43] According to Austria's SOLVIT centre, it was due to an increase in the number of cases in relation to the previous year and to the closure of some very old cases, especially concerning Slovakian workers working in Austria.

Among the weaknesses of the SOLVIT network are its scarce resources and limited legal expertise enabling the centres to carry out their tasks in a satisfactory way and to deliver independent legal analysis of the cases. Ensuring an adequate level of staffing and legal expertise is even more pressing if we take into account the increasing variety of cases that SOLVIT is asked to address. Although staffing in some SOLVIT centres improved in 2011, the overall staffing levels of the centres remain problematic. In addition, in almost all SOLVIT centres, the staff members have other responsibilities as well, which sometimes take priority over SOLVIT tasks. Currently only 14 SOLVIT centres are adequately staffed.[44] The centres in France, Germany and the UK in particular face a lack of experienced staff in light of the high caseload. In order to solve this problem, the Commission services are consider proposing, together with the member states, minimum staffing requirements.

Since 2009, the Commission also has given SOLVIT centres the possibility to request legal advice from the lawyers working in 'Your Europe' and an increased number of SOLVIT centres used this option during 2011. In future, the Commission will also continue to provide informal legal advice (through a help desk placed in DG MARKT, but with SOLVIT contact points in other DGs), within a targeted time of two weeks maximum, as well as organise regular legal training sessions and meetings between SOLVIT staff and Commission policy officers.[45] SOLVIT centres are also encouraged by the Commission to build their own networks with the national administration in order to obtain specialised legal advice. Furthermore, when the informal legal advice provided by the Commission does not lead to satisfactory results (because the national authority refuses to comply with EU law) or when the issue in question is too complex to be clarified by informal legal advice within the two-week deadline, the Commission could advise the SOLVIT centres to close the case as unresolved and, when appropriate, decide to pursue the case in EU Pilot (for 'EU Pilot', see chapter 6, section 6.2.2.2).

---

[44] Namely, Austria, Bulgaria, Estonia, Italy, Latvia, Malta, Poland, Portugal, Romania, Slovakia, Slovenia, Spain, Sweden and Liechtenstein. See European Commission, "Making the Single Market deliver: Annual governance check-up 2011", 2011.

[45] During 2011, two workshops and two training sessions were organised and a large number of SOLVIT centres also participated in the Single Market Forum in Krakow in October 2011.

5.1.3 An overview of the SOLVIT business cases

Attracting business cases in SOLVIT remains a key priority for the Commission, as the number of business cases has remained relatively stable and low in comparison to the increased number of citizen cases since the network was set up (Figure 7).[46] In 2010, 167 businesses cases were recorded out of a total number of 1363 cases (Figure 7 below).

Figure 7. Number of business cases requesting support from SOLVIT, 2007-10

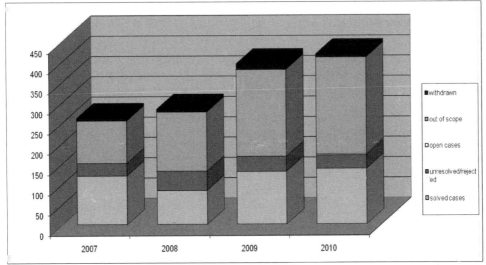

Source: European Commission, DG Internal Market and Services, Evaluation of SOLVIT, Final Report, November 2011.

In order to promote the use of SOLVIT by businesses, in 2009 the European Commission produced a Strategy Paper to guide SOLVIT centres on how they could develop activities in a coherent way to increase the awareness of businesses about SOLVIT.[47] Some SOLVIT centres are

---

[46] The share of business cases handled by SOLVIT each year in the period 2003 to 2010 in relation to the total number of cases was: 33% (2003), 34% (2004), 29% (2005), 31% (2006), 18% (2007), 14% (2008), 11% (2009) and 12% (2010).

[47] See European Commission (2009) Strategy Paper, "Increasing awareness about SOLVIT among businesses users", 2009. The Strategy Paper was built on the results of the European Businesses Test Panel, which found that 80% of businesses that had not previously heard of SOLVIT would be willing to use it if they required such services. The document seeks a comprehensive approach to delivering awareness-raising activities, developing a more effective web presence,

developing various forms of promoting their activities among business so as to attract more business cases.[48] Although a number of effective means have been developed by some SOLVIT centres to promote their activities towards business, many centres have not fully mainstreamed an approach to the extent envisaged by the Strategy Paper. This may be due to a lack of resources to develop an appropriate strategy and implement activities and then to deal with the potential increase in case load. However, it should also be noted that public awareness campaigns sometimes have a negative side effect by bringing in non-SOLVIT business cases.

On other hand, we must keep in mind that the SOLVIT network is not always an appropriate or/and attractive problem-solving system to address cross-border business problems arising from the incorrect or inaccurate application of the single market rules. Indeed, sometimes it is difficult for SOLVIT to deal with business cases, for various reasons:

- Given that considerable sums of money or compensation are often sought by companies, they may prefer to employ their own lawyers using formal channels offering more leverage.

- Business cases are often seen as complex (often involving harmonisation or technical market access issues).

- National administrations may choose to ignore informal legal advice which puts businesses off.

- As SOLVIT is a governmental organisation, businesses may wrongly believe that it is not an independent network and this may lead some companies to feel uncomfortable with SOLVIT if they require support in areas such as taxation.

We observe that the low number of business SOLVIT cases is not only due to a lack of awareness within the business community, but also, to some extent, to SOLVIT being a network for settling cross-border disputes

---

partnerships with umbrella business organisations and cooperation with institutional partners as well as delivering quick and effective services for business.

[48] For instance, Sweden has been notably successful in targeting advertising at businesses through various means including website links, awareness booklets with examples of successful SOLVIT outcomes and organising seminars with stakeholders. Other SOLVIT centres have been promoting SOLVIT among businesses by placing advertisements in business newspapers (Germany), developing relations with chambers of commerce (Poland) and promoting public transport advertisement campaigns (Czech Republic).

informally and for free. After all, these properties are more likely to attract citizen and SME cases. For that reason, the European Commission is attempting to enhance the level of awareness of SOLVIT among SMEs. Strengthening relations with the European Enterprise Network should improve the awareness of SOLVIT among SMEs and help to attract more cases. In effect, in 2011, we could observe an increase in business cases (Figure 8), but the number remains low compared with the number of citizen cases (214 closed business cases were recorded).

Figure 8. Closed SOLVIT business cases by area, 2011

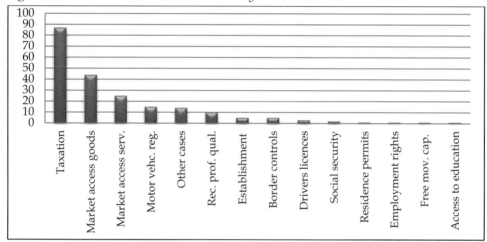

Source: Data made available to the authors by the European Commission.

Taxation (41% or 87 cases), followed by problems in the area of free movement of goods (21% or 44 cases) and services (12% or 25 cases) clearly remain the key issues when doing cross-border business within the internal market (Figure 8).

From the 87 taxation cases concluded by SOLVIT in 2011, 73 were closed as solved, 13 as unresolved and one case was rejected (Figure 9). A closer look at the taxation business cases indicates that the vast majority of the cases involve cross-border problems related with value-added tax (VAT) reimbursement. In particular, they involve situations where the application for refunding the VAT charged must be submitted to the local authorities of another member state where the company is not established. Notably it is about delays on the reimbursement of the VAT to companies that imported goods or exported goods and services from that member state. The rules governing VAT refunds to taxable persons not established in the member state of refund are laid down by Directive 2008/9/EC.[49] In a large majority of the cases, the case was successfully solved after the intervention of the SOLVIT centres, and the VAT was refunded to the companies.

Figure 9. Outcome of taxation-related business cases handled by SOLVIT, 2011

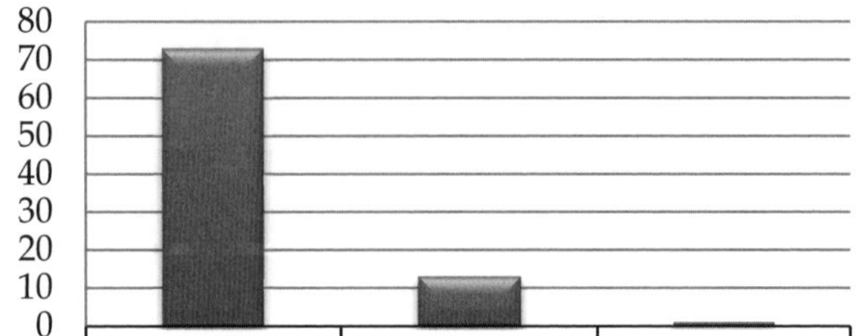

	Solved cases	Unresolved cases	Rejected cases
▣ Solution rate - Taxation Business SOLVIT cases - Total number 87 cases	73	13	1

Note: A total of 87 cases were submitted in 2011.

Source: Data made available to the authors by the European Commission.

The free movement of goods is the second main policy area in which SOLVIT handled business cases. Out of a total of 44 cases in this field in 2011, 36 were solved, six were unresolved and two were rejected (Figure 10 below).

---

[49] See Directive 2008/9/EC of 12 September 2008, laying down detailed rules for the value added tax, provided for in Directive 2006/112/EC, to taxable persons not established in the member state of refund but established in another member state. According to Art. 19 (2) of Directive 2008/9/EC, the member state of refund shall notify the applicant of its decision to approve or refuse the refund application within four months of its receipt. If the refund application is approved, the refund VAT shall be paid at the latest within 10 working days of the expiry deadline referred to in Art. 19 (2) (four months). If the member state of refund considers that it does not have all the relevant information, according to Art. 20 of Directive 2008/9/EC, it may request additional information within the four-month period referred to in Art. 19 (2).

Figure 10. Outcome of business cases in the area of free movement of goods handled by SOLVIT, 2011

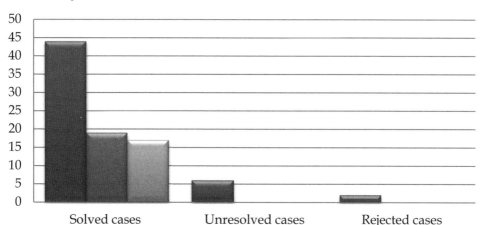

Note: A total of 44 cases were submitted in 2011.

Source: Data made available to the authors by the European Commission.

A large share of the cases (23) is related to the refusal by the authority in a member state to allow entry of a product that is not EU-regulated (non-harmonised area) or is only partially regulated at EU level (see Table 1). The reasons for the refusal of market access include the existence of different national standards, no notification of national technical standards to the European Commission according to the procedure laid down in Directive 98/34/EC, the imposition of national standards that are complementary to existing European standards and/or the imposition of different or extra testing and certification requirements. Some cases also involve national technical regulations that had been correctly notified to the European Commission, according to the 98/34/EC procedure and never received any kind of objection from the European Commission or the member states.

These cases clearly involve the correct application of Arts 34 and 36 TFEU and the principle of mutual recognition. Since free movement of goods is directly applicable to all member states, member states are obliged to accept products lawfully marketed in another member state and that are not subject to Union harmonisation (Art. 34 TFEU), unless very specific conditions are met (Art. 36 TFEU). This means that certain national technical barriers may be justified, while others may not.

Table 1. Number of SOLVIT closed business cases by sector and area (2011) – Free movement of goods

Products	Non-harmonised area*	Harmonised area	Total
Food	4	4	8
Fertilisers	3	1	4
Other products	8	4	12
Medicinal product	1	2	3
Motor vehicles	4	4	8
Pressure equipment	1	1	2
Pyrotechnic articles	1	0	1
Construction	1	2	3
Toys	0	2	2
Total	23	20	43[50]

* We have included in the non-harmonised area all the cases referring to products that are partially regulated at EU level, but the aspect that was at the origin of the complaint falls outside the scope of the directive. This is the case, for example, of some SOLVIT cases related to components, systems and parts of motor vehicles, pressure equipment, pyrotechnic articles and some foodstuffs. Moreover, it should be noted that it is not always easy to classify the product as being harmonised or non-harmonised at EU level, because sometimes the case description is formulated in an imprecise or unclear way by the Lead/Home Centre. For that reason, the table above should be read with caution.

Source: Data made available to the authors by the European Commission.

Moreover, according to the principle of mutual recognition, a product lawfully marketed in one member state and not subject to Union harmonisation or falling outside the scope of a directive of harmonised EU legislation, should be allowed to be marketed in any other member state, even when the product does not fully comply with the technical rules of the member state of destination. A member state can only refuse the marketing of a product if it can show that this is strictly necessary for the protection of, for example, public safety, health or environment and it must also

---

[50] One of the rejected cases is not included, because the product is not identified in the SOLVIT database.

demonstrate that its measure is the least trade-restrictive one.[51] Furthermore, to make the mutual recognition principle fully operational, the European Parliament and the Council adopted Regulation (EC) No 764/2008,[52] which establishes rules and procedures that should be followed by the national authorities when they intend to take restrictive measures which could hinder the free movement of a product lawfully marketed in another member state, and are not covered by harmonised rules at EU level. In particular, the Regulation concentrates on the burden of proof to the member states of importation. It thereby protects the company seeking market access by setting out the strict procedural requirements for denying mutual recognition and applying to administrative decisions based on a technical rule which has the direct or indirect effect of:

- the prohibition of placing a product on the market,

- the modification or additional testing of that product before it can be placed on the market or

- the withdrawal of that product.

Moreover, according to the Regulation, an evaluation of the need to apply a technical rule should be based on technical or scientific elements, proving the proportionality of the envisaged measure, should be notified to the enterprise concerned and can be legally challenged.

In the harmonised area (20 cases), the problems reported to SOLVIT involve mainly situations where the national regulations go beyond the relevant directive/regulation, by imposing additional requirements on products that had been certified in another member state and that comply with the essential requirements imposed by EU legislation.

Three complaints were also received by the SOLVIT centres related to cross-border problems faced by businesses when trying to place on the market or obtain the registration of motor vehicles, systems, components and separate technical units intended for such vehicles that are subject to

---

[51] See Pelkmans, (2012) for an extensive explanation and analysis. See also *Dassonville, C-8-74* and *Cassis (Rewe), C-120/78*.

[52] See Regulation (EC) No 764/2008 of the European Parliament and of the Council of 9 July 2008, laying down procedures relating to the application of certain national technical rules to products lawfully marketed in another member state and repealing decision No 3052/95/EC.

step-by-step type approval, according to Directive 2007/46/EC,[53] in another member state (see Table 1).

The sectors most affected are food (eight cases), motor vehicles (eight cases), fertilisers (four cases), construction products (three cases) and medicinal products (three cases) (see Table 1).

Free movement of services is also one of the main areas in which SOLVIT business cases occurred. In 2011, 25 were closed by the SOLVIT centres in this area, 20 were closed as solved, four as unresolved and one case was rejected (Figure 11).

Figure 11. Solution rate of SOLVIT business cases in the area of freedom to provide services, 2011

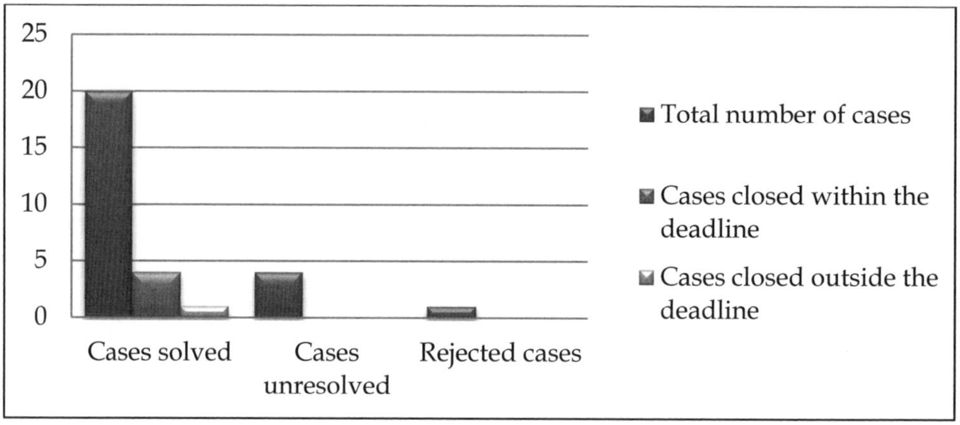

Source: Data made available to the authors by the European Commission.

The freedom to provide services comprises the elimination of all kinds of discrimination based on nationality as well as the prohibition of the obligation on the provider to have residence or an establishment in the territory of the member states where the service is provided. The member state in which the service is provided can only enforce its own requirements inasmuch as these are non-discriminatory, proportional and justified for reasons of public order, public safety, public health or environmental protection.

---

[53] Directive 2007/46/EC of the European Parliament and of the Council of 5 September 2007, establishing the framework for the approval of motor vehicles and their trailers, and of system, components and separate technical units intended for such vehicles.

In order to facilitate the freedom of establishment for providers in other member states and the freedom of provision of services between member states, two directives were enacted: the services Directive 2006/123/EC and the recognition of professional qualifications Directive 2005/36/EC.

The main problems presented by business in this area are precisely related to requirements conflicting with the services Directive 2006/123/EC,[54] mainly with Arts 15 and 16, and requirements conflicting with Directive 2005/36/EC[55] on the recognition of professional qualifications (Table 2).

Table 2. Number of business SOLVIT cases by sector (2011) – Free movement of services

Sectors	Number of cases by sector	Problem		
		Directive 2006/123/EC	Recognition of professional qualifications (Directive 2005/36/CE or other)	Other
Engineering	1	X	X	
Electricity, gas	4	X	X	Arts 56 and 57 TFEU ISO 9001/2008 Other
Transportation and storage	1			Euro-license
Tourism	2	X	X	Other
Telecommunications	2			Directive 2002/20/EC[a] Other
Food services activities	1	X		

---

[54] Directive 2006/123/EC of the European Parliament and of the Council of 12 December 2006 on Services in the internal market.

[55] Directive 2005/36/EC of the European Parliament and of the Council of 7 September 2005 on the recognition of professional qualifications.

Human health services	1			Action was brought before the national Constitutional Court
Construction	1			Directive 85/337/EEC of 27 June 2005[b]
Scientific research and development	1			Other
Financial and insurance activity	2			Directive 2009/103/EC[c] Arts 56, 57, 59 and 60 TFEU
Aviation	1			Regulation 1008/2008/EC[d]
IT and other communication services	2			Unresolved cases[e]
Others	1			Other (EN 60335-2-27; chapter IV of Directive 2001/95/EC)[f]
Agriculture, forestry and fishing	1			Other
Accounting, consultancy	2	X	X	
Temporary work	1			Directive 2008/104/EC[g]
Total	24[h]			

[a] Directive 2002/20/EC of the European Parliament and of the Council of 7 March 2002, on the authorisation of electronic communications networks and services.

[b] Directive 85/337/EEC of 27 June 2005 on the assessment of the effects of certain public and private projects on the environment.

[c] Directive 2009/103/EC of the European Parliament and of the Council of 16 September 2009, relating to insurance against civil liability in respect of the use of motor vehicles, and enforcement of the obligation to insure against such liability.

[d] Regulation (EC) No 1008/2008 of the European Parliament and of the Council of 24 September 2008 on common rules for the operation of air services in the Community (Recast).

[e] It is not clear from a reading of the Solvit cases what the problems are in these two cases.

[f] Directive 2001/95/EC of the European Parliament and of the Council of 3 December 2001 on general product safety.

[g] Directive 2008/104/EC of 19 November 2008 on temporary agency work.

[h] Rejected case not included.

Source: Data made available to the authors by the European Commission.

5.1.4 SOLVIT-Plus cases and Art. 258 TFEU

SOLVIT was set up to deal with 'individual' problems caused by the misapplication of internal market rules by a public administration. A typical SOLVIT case involves the misconduct by an administration when the national regulatory framework conforms to EU law. SOLVIT centres are required in principle to dismiss cases where the individual administrative problem results from the fact that the national regulatory structure does *not* conform to EU law. Nevertheless, some SOLVIT centres have developed a different practice, by dealing with cases where the internal market problem was, on the contrary, caused by a national barrier raised either by a specific regulation or by an unlawful administrative practice.

In such cases (referred to as 'SOLVIT-Plus' cases), SOLVIT centres resolved the individual problem by convincing the public administration not to apply the unlawful regulation or to move away from the unlawful practice. Moreover, the centre reports the case to the relevant national authorities in order to have the specific regulation amended or to have practices changed.

With SOLVIT-Plus cases, the SOLVIT centres have been playing a role that is complementary to the enforcement activities of the Commission under Art. 258 TFEU, by helping to resolve structural problems and to remove illicit regulatory barriers.[56]

5.1.5 SOLVIT and EU Pilot

In 2008, the Commission launched the Pilot project,[57] aimed at fostering a more efficient and effective dialogue between member states and the Commission when dealing with inquiries and complaints about national breaches of EU law. In others words, the idea is to improve the collaboration between the Commission and member states at the pre-

---

[56] The importance of this role played by SOLVIT has been acknowledged by the Commission in its 2007 Communication, "A Europe of results – Applying Community Law", where the Commission stresses the importance to reduce the recourse to infringement proceedings by fostering the use of alternative problem-solving mechanisms and preventive measures.

[57] EU Pilot was launched in April 2008, following the Commission Communication, "A Europe of results – Applying Community Law", COM(2007)502 final. See section 6.2.2.2 in chapter 6.

infringement stage, to act like a sort of pre-infringement information-gathering tool, facilitating the Commission's work.[58]

However, EU Pilot has become in fact a replacement for the informal phase of the infringement procedures and its scope is different from that of SOLVIT. It is not always easy for Commission services to decide which system should be used.[59] Indeed, Pilot, like SOLVIT, aims at providing an informal, rapid and effective solution to problems arising from the misapplication of EU law. To help the Commission services in this task, some criteria have been developed to decide whether the case should be referred by the Commission services to EU Pilot or to SOLVIT (see Table 3).

From our analysis of Table 3, we can conclude that the scope of SOLVIT is restricted to issues with a cross-border dimension that are related to the bad application of the internal market law and are *not* related to late or bad transposition of EU law or non-conformity with EU law. EU Pilot, by contrast, covers all areas of EU law, except specific problems raised in a cross-border context in the internal market, the intervention of EU Pilot in issues with a cross-border dimension related to internal market law is restricted to cases of non-conformity with EU law.

The involvement of the Commission also remains much larger in EU Pilot than in the case of SOLVIT, since the Commission is always involved at every step of the EU Pilot procedure and a copy of the member state response is sent to the Commission. By contrast, in the case of SOLVIT, all contacts always directly involve the complainant.

Although the criteria provide general guidance on whether a case should be referred to EU Pilot or SOLVIT, in practice it may be difficult to decide the best route for an individual case. This could be achieved through better cooperation between the two systems at Commission level. However, according to the SOLVIT evaluation report from November 2011, Commission officials and those responsible for the national SOLVIT centres suggest that at the moment there is not a particularly strong link between EU Pilot and SOLVIT at EU level. Moreover, SOLVIT centres stress the importance of submitting their unresolved cases to the Commission for consideration in EU Pilot. At present, when an unresolved SOLVIT case is

---

[58] We explore EU Pilot in more detail in sub-section 6.2.2.2, 'EU Pilot' in chapter 6.

[59] It should be noted that citizens and businesses do not submit cases directly to EU Pilot. The complaints are submitted to the Commission and then the Commission decides which system should be used.

sent to EU Pilot, often the legal analysis and evidence already collected by SOLVIT are ignored. However, one should avoid a duplication of efforts.[60]

Table 3. Criteria for deciding whether to submit cases to SOLVIT or EU Pilot

SOLVIT	EU PILOT
General coverage	**General coverage**
Specific problems raised in a cross-border context in the internal market	All areas of EU law except specific or general problems arising from cross-border issues in the internal market
More specific aspects of coverage	**More specific aspects of coverage**
Involves specific problems encountered by an individual or a business	Involves specific or general problems reported by individuals, commercial operators or interested organisations
Due to incorrect application of EU rules governing the functioning of the internal market within the meaning of Art. 26 (2) TFEU	Due to the incorrect application of EC rules outside the functioning of the internal market within the meaning of Art. 26 (2) TFEU or, exceptionally, that might merit further pursuit through EU Pilot having had some initial treatment in SOLVIT
By a member state public authority	By a member state public authority
Raises a cross-border issue	Does not raise a cross-border issue, except where it is clear from the start that it involves an issue of non-conformity of national law
Is not already subject to national legal proceedings	May already be subject to legal proceedings
Is not due to late or bad transposition of EU law or other non-conformity of member states law with the European law	May be due to non-conformity of national legislation with Community law, including such issues arising in the context of the internal market within the meaning of Art. 26 (2) TFEU

Source: European Commission, Evaluation of SOLVIT, Final Report, November 2011.

---

[60] Evaluation of SOLVIT, Final Report, November 2011.

There is a clear necessity to promote better links between EU Pilot and SOLVIT in terms of coordination, communication, filtering the cases and the creation of mechanisms to allocate transfer cases from one system to another. In order to do so, the Commission intends to promote the use of SOLVIT as the first instance to deal with individual cross-border problems resulting from a potential misapplication of EU law (subject to the complainants' previous approval) and establish a better information exchange between the SOLVIT, CHAP (a complaints handling system that registers complaints and inquiries on the application of EU law by a member state, set up by the European Commission in 2009) and EU Pilot.[61]

5.2 The European Consumer Centres Network

The European Consumer Centres Network (ECC-Net), an EU-wide network created in 2005,[62] focuses on cross-border business-to-consumers issues (B2C) (either in person or via distance purchase, mainly e-commerce).[63] It provides information to consumers, ensures that they are aware of their rights and gives support to consumers in the event of a complaint. The network comprises 29 centres (one in each of the 27 EU member states plus Iceland and Norway), under the supervision of the Directorate-General for Health and Consumers (DG SANCO) and financial management of the Executive Agency for Health and Consumers.

The main goal of the ECC-Net is to promote consumer confidence in the internal market. The full potential of the EU B2C internal market is still far from realised. In 2009, B2C markets in the EU represent 57% of the EU's GDP, but cross-border shopping only accounts for approximately 1.2% of the entire B2C market.[64] One of the main reasons preventing consumers from engaging in cross-border shopping is the difficulty to obtain effective redress in the event of a problem and the lack of information about the

---

[61] European Commission Working Document, "Reinforcing effective problem-solving in the Single Market: Unlocking SOLVIT's full potential at the occasion of its 10th anniversary".

[62] The ECC-Net results from the merger of the Euroguichets and the European Extra-Judicial Network (EEJ-Net).

[63] Business-to-Business issues and pure national cases fall outside the scope of the ECCs as well as cases involved in a governmental structure.

[64] Special Eurobarometer 298, "Consumer protection in the Internal Market", October 2008.

advantages/disadvantages and their rights when buying in other countries. In this context, the ECC-Net plays an important role by:

- providing information and advice to consumers on their rights,

- giving assistance to consumers in the resolution of their individual cross-border complaints and

- helping consumers whose complaints are not solved amicably to reach an agreement via an out-of-court alternative dispute resolution (ADR) mechanism.

ECCs do not have enforcement powers, which means that they can neither sanction the trader nor represent consumers in court or in an ADR scheme. However, in the cases where it is not possible to obtain an amicable solution with the trader, ECCs advise consumers on the appropriate ADR bodies, leading consumers to other more appropriate EU-wide networks (such as FIN-Net, SOLVIT and the European Judicial Network-EJN) in civil and commercial matters or proposing other ways to solve their problems (such as the European small claims procedure),[65] so as to try to avoid a lengthy and costly normal court procedure. By doing so, ECCs not only help consumers to solve their individual cross-border shopping problems, but also to ensure the observance of consumer rights granted by EU law.

Moreover, the ECC-Net also provides a valuable input for the European Commission on consumer policy issues, since it is in a unique position to know what are the main problems faced by consumers when shopping cross-border.

The evidence points to a growing demand for the services offered by the Network. Over the period 2005 to 2009, the number of cases handled by the ECCs rose by 25%.[66] In 2010, ECC-Net received 71,292 cases (15% more than in 2009), of which 41.6% of the cases were closed after an amicable settlement was obtained.[67]

However, each year a significant number of cases handled by the ECCs are closed without reaching any solution (39% in 2009 and 42.6% in 2010) or are transferred to other organisations (13% in 2009 and 15.5% in

---

[65] Regulation (EC) No 861/2007 of the European Parliament and of the Council of 11 July 2007 establishing an European small claims procedure.

[66] The European Consumer Centres Network, Fifth Anniversary Report 2005-2009.

[67] The European Consumer Centres Network 2010 Annual Report, 2011.

2010). In 2010, 58.5% (900) of the transferred cases were remitted to out-of-court settlement bodies. This means that the ECC-Net's capacity to facilitate redress is constrained not only by the willingness of the traders to engage with the ECCs in the resolution of consumer complaints, but also by external factors such as the efficiency of ADR systems across the Europe.

The ECCs deal with an extensive range of cross-border consumer issues such as transport, package holidays, timeshare, e-commerce, non-delivered or defective goods and unfair commercial practices, among others. In more than half of the cases (56.2%) handled by the ECC centres in 2010, the product or service was purchased on-line. Transport remains the sector with more complaints dealt with by the ECC-Net (33.2%), and 57% of them were related to air passengers' rights. The other sectors with a large number of complaints were recreation and cultural services (23.7%) and restaurants, hotel and accommodation (11.5%). A large part of the consumers' problems concerned the quality of the product or the service (29.5%), the delivery (23.7%), the contract terms (12.2%) and the price and payment (10.5%).

5.3   Commission Scoreboards

The Commission has maintained the Internal Market Scoreboard for 15 years now, publishing the results twice a year. Although a range of issues concerning the internal market has been dealt with in the Scoreboard over the years, the permanent feature is the regular reporting on transposition and application of EU (internal market) law, including infringement records. It is therefore a crucial source for any insight in the proper functioning of the single market. But its significance goes much further. With the careful and regular monitoring of implementation and application by the member states, strategies to improve the initially poor records of many EU countries have been based on the indicators of the Scoreboard and are receiving targeted publicity with the help of the Scoreboard. The status of each member state is easy to discern from the Scoreboard and there is no way 'to hide'. Poor records of certain member states lead to criticism inside these countries and attract the attention of investors and business more generally. The Scoreboard is therefore more than just a tool – it positively helps to improve transposition and enforcement.

The latest Scoreboard is from September 2011 (No. 23),[68] not counting the February 2012 Single Market Governance paper[69] of the Commission (in which the Scoreboard of spring 2012 is incorporated). The standard for proper implementation by member states has become stricter over time and the target of the 'transposition deficit' of all 27 member states has been 1% for a number of years. A new proposal from the Commission is to lower the transposition deficit to 0.5%. In the Stockholm European Council of 2001, the target transposition deficit was set at 1.5%, which was seen as tough at the time. The transposition deficit is defined as the percentage share of internal market directives not yet notified or implemented by member states of the total number of directives which should have been notified by the deadline. On 30 April 2011, the latter total amounted to 1,525 directives.[70] Figure 12 shows the deficit over the last four years, which has been below 1% for three years, yet is creeping upwards again in 2011.

The Scoreboard rightly points at individual member states and shows whether they do well or fail. This is good for bringing pressure on EU countries to make greater efforts. For the present report, it seems less useful to focus on individual member states as, over time, there is quite some fluctuation in these figures. In May 2011, there were no less than 16 member states above the 1% target transposition deficit, with Austria, Poland and the Czech Republic showing transposition delays for 26–31 directives, which is worrying. Given these delays, the European Council

---

[68] See European Commission, Internal Market Scoreboard No. 23, "Together for new growth", September 2011.

[69] European Commission, "Making the Single Market deliver – Annual Governance check-up 2011", Working Document, 2012.

[70] Note that, in addition, 1,347 EU (Council/EP) regulations govern the internal market. The transposition deficit does not apply to these regulations, of course (as they have direct legal effect on all economic agents). However, by focusing solely on the directives (and their transposition deficit), one ignores a significant change over time in the weight of directives versus regulations. Thus, in Scoreboard No. 10 (May 2002), it appears that the internal market at the time was governed by 1,497 directives and only 299 regulations. So, nine years later another 1,000 regulations have been added, whereas the total number of directives has barely increased (mainly because many families of directives have been consolidated and some have been deleted; others have been replaced by regulations). Therefore, a given transposition deficit is *relatively* less problematic in 2012 than it was 10 years ago. For more details, see section 8.7 in chapter 8. (Selective shift from internal market directives to EU regulations).

has set a 'zero tolerance' for transposition overdue by more than two years. Over 2009-11, the number of 'overdue' directives not yet transposed (in all EU countries) fell from 22 to only three and this refers to four EU countries.

Figure 12. Average transposition deficit from November 2007 to November 2011

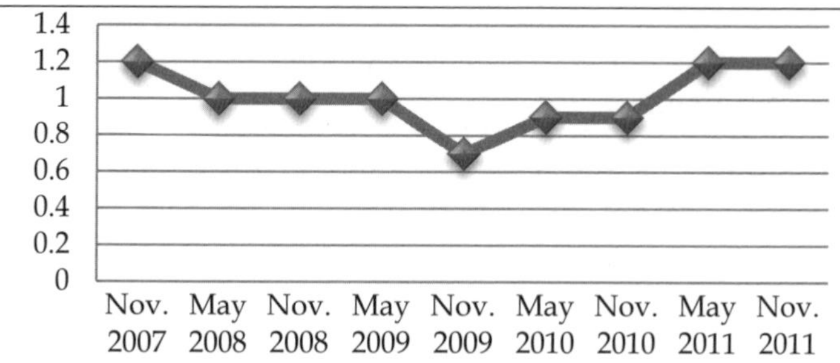

	Nov. 2007	May 2008	Nov. 2008	May 2009	Nov. 2009	May 2010	Nov. 2010	May 2011	Nov. 2011
Average transposition deficit	1.2	1	1	1	0.7	0.9	0.9	1.2	1.2

Source: European Commission, "Making the Single Market deliver – Annual Governance check-up 2011", Working Document, 2012.

The 'compliance' deficit is about incorrect transposition: the percentage share of incorrectly transposed directives from the total number of transposed directives, per member state. The average compliance deficit stands at 0.8%. Also for this indicator, the Commission proposes to have a 0.5% target. What is surely worrying is the combination of a high transposition and a high compliance deficit. This is the case for Belgium (together, 3.1% of the total of directives), Italy (idem, 3.2%) and Poland (idem, 3.3%). If one also knows that Belgium and Italy are no. 1 and no. 3 in the hit list of pending infringement cases, with 101 and 79 cases, respectively, the overall picture of internal market enforcement in these countries is outright poor. For Belgium, the comparison with (say) November 2007 is painful because its number of pending infringement cases increased by no less than 53% (!), whereas in Italy the number decreased by 41%. Indeed, all other member states have reduced their number of pending cases in this period.

Finally, the Internal Market Scoreboard publishes the 'fragmentation factor', an overall indicator of 'legal gaps'. This factor is defined as the percentage share of the directives not (yet) transposed in one or more EU member states of the total number of directives that should have been transposed by that date. This is quite different from the 'transposition deficit', because the latter is averaged between member states – i.e. in 2011 (May and November), it stood at 1.2%, as shown in Figure 12 – whereas the former results from adding up all directives that, somewhere in the internal market, are not yet transposed. The fragmentation factor fell from November 2007 (8%) to 6% in May 2011. In the second half of 2011, member states reduced the number of directives remaining to be transposed and have improved their enforcement performance with respect to long-overdue directives. However, the transposition target of 1% was missed for the second time since May 2008, and the average delay for transposition has increased to almost eight months.[71]

For business, especially for European-wide business strategy, the fragmentation factor needs to be as low as possible. Nevertheless, the Commission employs an exaggerated interpretation in the Scoreboard, making the internal market look more fragmented than it really is. "*Instead of the Internal Market covering all Member States, it remains much smaller and fragmented. Consequently, the economic interests of all Member States already suffer if one Member State does not deliver*" (p. 18, underlining in original). The Commission adds: "*In other words, the Internal Market is operating at only 94% of its potential*" and ..." *(T)his penalises all Member States, their citizens and businesses.*"

But, of course, the internal market is not "much smaller and fragmented" in each and every case, and it is far from obvious that 'all' member states and businesses are penalised. If one country A has not yet transposed, there are still 26 other EU countries, and a 'European-wide' strategy can surely be employed quite successfully. With two or three countries, this may well be true, too. Few companies operate literally in all 27 member states, knowing that the EU comprises many small economies. Also, there are many other reasons why operating in all 27 countries may be less straightforward than implicitly suggested by the Commission, such as fixed entry costs in terms of marketing and after-sale services, local languages, (costly) regulatory heterogeneity between EU countries in issues under national legislative powers, patents (which are national in the EU), currencies other than the euro,[72] etc. Therefore, to hold that the internal market is operating at only 94% of its capacity is an artificial approach not

---

[71] European Commission, "Making the Single Market deliver – Annual Governance check-up 2011", Working Document, 2012.

[72] See Richard E. Baldwin (2006). In this work on the economic impact of the euro, the author found that the euro made it possible for European business to enter smaller country markets that otherwise would have remained too marginal for them. See also Ottaviano & Ireo (2007).

reflecting economic reality for business. This is not to say that the fragmentation factor is irrelevant; rather, that it better be moderated to what it should mean.[73]

The Consumer Scoreboard exists since 2008 and is published twice a year: the Consumer Conditions Scoreboard in the spring and the Consumer Markets Scoreboard in the autumn. The triple purpose of the Consumer Scoreboard is to identify whether consumer markets are working for the consumer, tracking the integration of the retail single market and monitoring national consumer conditions. The latter two objectives are related to the 'Conditions' Scoreboard; the former to the 'Markets' Scoreboard. Malfunctioning markets frustrate the working of the single market, too, including – in the final analysis – the growth and productivity function of the EU internal market. Such malfunctioning can have many reasons, but one amongst many can be improper enforcement. The Conditions Scoreboard is particularly geared to indicators tracing possible enforcement issues, amongst other factors.

The Consumer Scoreboard deals with cross-border issues, e.g. cross-border on-line purchases and the reticence of European consumers to make such purchases in view of the widespread perception that redress options are weak or even failing. For the purposes of the present report, it is not always clear whether such difficulties are due to internal market enforcement failures or to other 'barriers' such as fear among retailers about credit cards or national bank cards or other market issues related to guarantees or transport.

The Market Monitoring in the Consumer Market Scoreboard, based on the Market Performance Indicator (MPI), differs from the exercise conducted by DG ECFIN of the Commission on 'malfunctioning markets' in the single market. The MPI is entirely based on how consumers experience the market working for them, including transparency (ease of comparing goods/services), trust in consumer protection, experience with problems and complaints and reporting of consumer satisfaction. These

---

[73] Thus, one might just as well suggest the opposite extreme for the 'fragmentation factor'. If in May 2011 there are 1,525 directives, then full transposition must imply 1,525 x 27 = 41,175 transpositions in member states. The 90 directives (Scoreboard, no. 23, p. 18) not yet transposed in at least one member state should be multiplied by the number of 'late' EU countries, for each case separately, and then added; the fragmentation factor is then the percentage share of that sum over 41,175. It is unlikely that this factor would reach even 2%.

aspects are broken down further (e.g. ease of switching, choice, etc.). Also, price divergences between national markets are studied with the support of national statistical offices and a considerable number of significant price disparities (especially for services, but not only) are found, which points to fragmentation which seems sustainable. However, whether that is due to enforcement questions, is anything but clear from this Scoreboard. In contrast, the DG ECFIN Market Monitoring seeks to identify 'malfunctioning markets' on the basis of indicators about regulation, 'integration' (vs. fragmentation) of that market (in the EU), competition and innovation and these are inspected (with economic indicators) in considerable depth (Ilzkovitz et al., 2007). But again, rather than inspecting enforcement issues in (EU and national implementation of EU) regulation, the indicators and analysis are entirely economic.

In the Consumer Conditions Scoreboard, the Commission makes use of a Consumer Conditions Index, made up of 12 indicators, five of them about enforcement. However, these 'national enforcement indicators' are not clearly referring to EU-wide or cross-border issues of enforcement and are therefore difficult to interpret for the purpose of the present report. They typically measure e.g. the number of inspections and laboratory tests, the number of compliance checks and notifications of a 'serious risk' (for the EU alert system) of goods and measures of the corrective remedies by authorities (like product withdrawal or injunctions, etc.). Undoubtedly, a good deal of these inspections or compliance indicators is relevant as they are often likely to be based on EU legislation, but there is no way of establishing the EU-wide significance of these enforcement efforts or possible weaknesses in them.

6. Formal Infringement Procedures

6.1 The 'classical' EU administrative procedure for enforcing EU law

The member states of the European Union are obliged to take measures ensuring that EU legal rules can be applied in domestic law (Art. 4(3) TEU).[74] Thus, one of the most important obligations of the Member States in the context of EU accession is to integrate in their own legal order the legal rules of the EU. This obligation explicitly includes the duty to ensure compliance of domestic rules with EU legal rules and also to apply the latter correctly.[75]

The Treaty on the Functioning of the EU (TFEU) provides various mechanisms for ensuring compliance with EU law. Of these, the procedure for infringement by member states of their obligations under EU law, which is regulated in Art. 258 TFEU (ex Art. 226 EC), is probably the most important contribution that EU law has made to the construction of a legal model of regional integration. Art. 258 TFEU grants the European Commission, as "guardian of the treaties",[76] the right to initiate infringement proceedings against member states that have failed to fulfil a

---

[74] Article 4 (3) TEU provides: "The member states shall take any appropriate measure, general or particular, to ensure fulfilment of the obligations arising out of the Treaties or resulting from the acts of the institutions of the European Union."

[75] The necessity for EU law to be obeyed was expressed by the CJEU more than 40 years ago in Case 6/6, *Costa v. ENEL*.

[76] As 'guardian of treaties', the European Commission shall ensure the implementation and correct application of EU law into the internal law of the member states, and, under, certain circumstances, it can bring to the Court of Justice, an action against a member state, if it finds that the state has not fulfilled its obligations under the treaties (Art. 17 (1) TEU).

treaty obligation. Through this mechanism for finding infringements of member states obligations under the treaties, the Commission ascertains that member states do not exercise powers that they have voluntarily delegated to the EU. The competence of introducing an appeal to involve state liability when they do not fulfil one or more of their obligations is reserved to the European Commission, according to Art. 258 TFEU.[77]

Art. 258 TFEU states: "if the Commission considers that a member state failed to fulfil any of its obligations, under this Treaty, the Commission issues a reasoned notification on the matter, after giving that state the opportunity to comment. If the state in question does not comply with the notification within the deadline set by the Commission, then the Commission may go to the Court of Justice."

Although, the Treaty speaks "of infringement of an obligation under this Treaty" (Art. 258 TFEU), these concepts are not defined in the Treaty. In the absence of a definition in the Treaty, the CJEU has established that a breach of the obligations is any infringement, by any state authority, of mandatory rules and principles of EU law. Whether it involves the provisions of constituent or modifying treaties, international agreements binding the EU, or general principles of law guaranteed by EU law, is not important.[78] The court also stated that the inconsistent behaviour of a member state may consist in an action, inaction or omission.[79]

---

[77] The principal enforcement actions before the CJEU are actions brought either by the Commission on behalf of the EU or by another member state than that which has failed to fulfil its Treaty obligations (Arts 258 and 259 TFEU, respectively). Under these enforcement provisions, neither natural nor legal persons can bring actions against member states. In fact, the TFEU does not provide for natural or legal persons to take direct action against member states before the CJEU. By contrast, member states can be made responsible for actions of its citizens (see C-265/95, *Commission v France*). Furthermore, it should be noted that, under the doctrine of 'direct effect', a member state may be liable to an individual (see the Cases *Francoviche* C-6/90 and *Factortame*, C-213/89).

[78] The breach of European law must be in respect of "a pre-existing, specific and precise obligation". In essence, it will refer to a breach of a Treaty provision, binding secondary legislation or a general principle of EU law. See Case 7/71, *Commission v. France*.

[79] Ibid.

The literature distinguishes five types of infringement, which can occur in the implementation of the EU law and against which the Commission may take action (see Figure 13):

a. **Violations of treaty provisions, regulations and decisions.** The provisions of treaties, Regulations[80] and Decisions[81] are directly applicable and, therefore, do not have to be incorporated into national law. In this case, non-compliance may take the form of not or incorrect applying and enforcing of the European obligations.

b. **Non-transposition of directives.** Directives are not directly applicable; they need to be incorporated into national law. The member states have discretionary power to choose the most effective means (form and methods) of implementation of EU Directives;[82] [83]

c. **Incorrect legal implementation[84] of directives.** The transposition of the directives may be incorrect. The Member States' transposition of EU legislation should be in absolute compliance with the requirements of those acts in the field. In this case, non-compliance with EU law takes the form of either incomplete or incorrect incorporation of directives into national law.

d. **Improper application of directives.** In this case the legal implementation of the directive is correct and complete, but it is not applied in actual practice. Non-compliance in this case involves the active violation of taking conflicting national measures or the passive failure to

---

[80] Treaty provisions and regulations are generally binding and directly applicable.

[81] Decisions are administrative acts aimed at specific individuals, companies or governments for which they are binding.

[82] According to the doctrine of the *'effect utile'*, the member states have to choose the most effective means for the transposition of the directives in their national legal system.

[83] Apart from the obligation of the member states to transpose EU directives in their own national law in absolute accordance with the requirements of these acts, member states also have the obligation to notify the Commission of national regulations transposing EU acts. This obligation is mentioned in most cases, in the final provisions of EU directives.

[84] Implementation refers to "what happens after a bill becomes a law" (Bardach, 1977) or, in the words of Barret (Barret, 2004), to the process of "translating policy into action". A similar, but slightly different concept is that of "compliance". Compliance refers to "a state of conformity or identity between an actor's behaviour and a specified rule" (Raustiala & Slaughter, 2002). It thus focuses less on the process than on the outcome of implementation.

invoke the obligations of the directive. The latter also includes failures to effectively enforce EU law, by taking positive actions against the violators, as well as failure to ensure adequate remedies/redress vis-à-vis the individuals for the infringement of their rights. The member states are obliged to ensure the exact enforcement of the transposing provisions.[85]

e. **Non-compliance with CJEU judgments**. Non-compliance in this case refers to the failure of member states to execute court judgments by remedying the issue, as determined by the CJEU in a previous judgment.

Figure 13. Infringements in the implementation process of the EU law

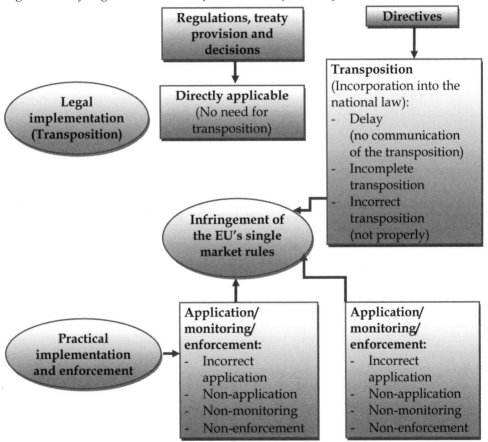

---

[85] From the analysis of the jurisprudence of the CJEU, we could conclude that the reason for the Commission complaints often is the inadequate implementation of EU legislation, and not the incomplete transposition or its non-transposition (see Table 4 below).

It should also be noted that the Commission has broad discretionary power to decide which infringements to pursue under Art. 258 TFEU. The CJEU has recognised that it is for the Commission to decide whether to bring proceedings concerning the application of EU law.[86] Recently, however, the Commission established criteria reflecting the seriousness of the alleged breach of EU law by setting three priorities:

-    Infringements undermining the foundations of the rule of law;

-    Infringements undermining the smooth functioning of the Community's legal system; and

-    Infringements consisting in the failure to transpose or correctly transpose directives, which can deprive large segments of the public access to EU law. [87]

6.2   Stages of the infringement procedure of EU law (Art. 258 TFEU)

There is no consensus in the specialised literature about the stages/phases of the procedure for finding the infringements by member states of the obligations assumed under the treaties, regulated in Arts 258 and 260 TFEU.[88]

We distinguish three main stages, which in turn comprise several sub-actions, namely an administrative stage, a pre-litigation stage and a judicial stage, the latter of which is of a more contentious nature. The broad picture of Figure 14 should help the reader to appreciate the entire procedure. Note that average durations of the various stages (together) are indicated in the figure as well as the percentage share of cases resolved in the respective stages.

---

[86] See case C-422/92, Commission v. Germany, 1995 E.C.R.I – 1097.

[87] See Commission Communication "Better Monitoring the Application of Community Law", Brussels 11.12.2002, COM (2002) 725 final.

[88] E.g. see Graig & de Burca, (2009). According to them, "the procedure of finding the infringement by the member states of obligations assumed, under the EC Treaty, can be divided into four distinct phases: the negotiation from the initial pre-contentious stage, the official notification on that alleged violation, via a letter from the Commission, the issuance of a reasoned notice from the Commission, sent to the State in question and the final stage referral to the Court of Justice, by the Commission."

Figure 14. Formal enforcement in case of infringement

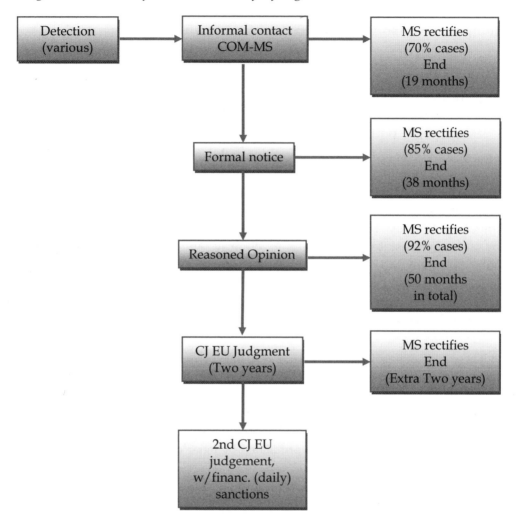

A few remarks on each stage follow below.

6.2.1 The administrative stage

6.2.1.1 The reasoned opinion by the Commission (Art. 258 TFEU)

Every time that the European Commission has serious reasons to believe that a member state has failed to fulfil its obligation under the treaties, it may initiate an infringement procedure for the breach of EU law, under Art. 258 TFEU.

The administrative and the pre-litigation stages must be completed before proceedings in the CJEU are undertaken. In effect, the administrative and pre-litigation stages:

- enable the Commission to ascertain the precise nature and extent of the infringement alleged,
- provide the Member State concerned with an essential guarantee with respect to its rights of defence and
- give both parties the opportunity of clarifying in cooperation with one another sometimes complex legal analysis, thus reaching an amicable solution.

The procedure under Art. 258 TFEU is initiated by the Commission in response to a complaint of a member state, a national or on its own initiative. Initially, the Commission investigates the possibility of a breach by a member state of its duty to comply with its obligations.[89] Such suspicions can be triggered by different sources: complaints presented by legal[90] or natural persons,[91] by own initiatives of the Commission,[92] from petitions[93] and questions[94] by the European Parliament and from the non-communication of the transposition of directives by the member states.

---

[89] These obligations, as mentioned above, may arise under the treaties, under secondary legislation or via agreements made by the EU with third countries under Art. 218 (1) TFEU.

[90] For example, companies, corporations and non-governmental organisations.

[91] The complaint can be drawn up in any official language of the European Union, is exempt from taxes and can be formulated by letter or using the standard form made available by the Commission.

[92] For example, based on evidence resulting from the annual reports on the situation of compliance with EU legal rules that member states are obliged to prepare.

[93] The European Parliament has a Committee on Petitions, which serves to receive such complaints from European citizens and from companies, organisations or associations with headquarters in the European Union (Art. 227 TFEU). Some of these petitions are submitted to the Commission for resolution and after analyzing them, the Commission may conclude that a member state has not complied with obligations under EU legal rules.

[94] The European Parliament, in exercising its control competences, may address questions to the Commission. Based on these questions, the Commission can take notice that a possible breach of EU law by a member state had occurred and can decide to open an infringement procedure under Art. 258 TFEU.

Any natural or legal person, who wants to complain about the violation of an EU legal rule by a member state could do so. Such person doesn't need to have any interest in that action or been directly injured. The only condition for admitting the complaint is that it relates to the violation of an EU legal rule by a member state. However, the procedure is not intended to offer people a way to appeal, but is designed as an objective mechanism to ensure compliance by the member state with EU law. Once the complaint is presented, it is recorded in a register kept by the General Secretariat of the Commission and the complainant receives a notification with the number of the complaint. Within a year, the Commission has to close the case or respond positively to the request by initiating the next stage. The complainant is then informed by the competent Directorate General in the field, on the action taken by the Commission, in response to his complaint.

If the Commission has reasons to believe that there is a case to answer, then the Directorate General responsible for the Union policy in question will write a letter to the member state suspected of violating its obligations under EU law.

6.2.1.2 The formal letter of notice (Art. 258 TFEU)

The administrative stage consists of a mutual exchange of views between the Commission and the member state, and also allows the delimitation of the scope of the future action brought before the CJEU. This phase aims to allow the member state concerned to justify its position or to persuade it to comply with the treaty requirements.

Whilst this is an informal stage, member states are under a duty to cooperate with the Commission.[95]

From the data available on member states' non-compliance with EU law, provided by the annual reports of the Commission on the monitoring of the application of EU law (see Table 4 and Figures 14 and 15), we conclude that most infringement proceedings are closed at this early stage of the procedure.[96] That could be explained, among other reasons, by a) the fact that member states usually try to avoid costly and lengthy judicial proceedings in the CJEU, b) the great number of infringement cases

---

[95] See Case 375/92, *Commission v. Spain.*

[96] See Figure 14 above. For a comparative picture over 2006–10, see Figure 16 below.

characterised by "non-communication" of the transposition of the directives into domestic law (see Figure 12) as well as c) the success of the negotiations between the Commission and the member states during the administrative stage, e.g. eliminating eventual problems of misinterpretation of EU law by member states.

Table 4. Closure decisions adopted in 2010 by stage

Stage of the procedure	Number of closures	Character of infringement	
		Non-communication	Other than non-communication
Before sending formal notice (Art. 258 TFEU)	431	0	431
Before sending reasoned opinion (Art. 258 TFEU)	870	558	312
Before referral to Court of Justice (Art. 258 TFEU)	269	139	130
Before lodging the application before the Court (Art. 258 TFEU)	27	9	18
Withdrawal	45	28	17
Before sending of formal notice (Art. 260 TFEU)	77	30	47
Before sending of reasoned opinion ex. Art. 228 TEC	44	23	21
Before second referral to Court of Justice (Art. 260 TFEU)	11	4	7
Before lodging the application before the Court of Justice (Art. 260 TFEU)	3	1	2
After judgement of the Court of Justice	2	0	2
TOTAL	**1,779**	**792**	**987**

Figure 15. Closure decisions adopted in 2010 by stage (in percentage)

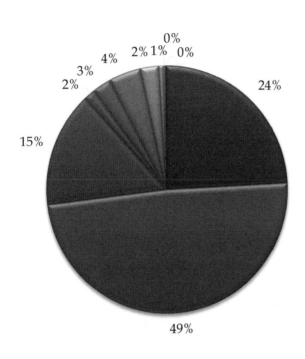

- Before sending formal notice -Art. 258 TFEU (24.23%)
- Before sending reasoned opinion - Art. 258 TFEU (48.90%)
- Before referral to the Court of Justice - Art. 258 TFEU (15.12%)
- Before lodging the application before the Court - Art. 258 TFEU (1.52%)
- Withdrawal (2.53%)

- Before sending formal notice -Art. 260 TFEU (4.33%)
- Before sending reasoned opinion ex art. 228 TEC (2.47%)
- Before second referral to Court of Justice - Art. 260 TFEU (0.62%)
- Before lodging the application before the Court - Art. 260 TFEU (0.17%)
- After Judgment of Court of Justice - Art. 260 TFEU (0.11%)

The procedure is initiated by the European Commission, sending a formal letter to the member state likely to have infringed EU law. The role of this 'letter of formal notice' is to delimit the subject matter; it invites the member state to submit its observations, collect information and eliminate any possible misunderstanding of the Commission.[97] The letter informs the member state of the Commission's position that there is a breach of an obligation under the Treaty and requests the member state to submit its comments on its alleged non-compliant behaviour. It must also explain

---

[97] "In practice, it frequently happens that in many cases the alleged infringement of EU law was due to shortcomings in translating national acts or to their misinterpretation.

what the EU law infringement is, contains a summary of the objections of the Commission and also sets a time limit during which the member state has the opportunity to make its observations.[98]

It should be noted that the formal letters, contrary to what the name suggests, are not part of the official proceedings. They are considered a preliminary stage, which gives the member state the opportunity to regularise its position and allows the Commission to collect information. For this reason, the formal letters are only made official if they refer to cases where member states have not accomplished their obligation of communicating the transposition of directives within the given time-limit.[99] The member state concerned, normally, has between one and two months in which to respond to the formal letter and can indicate, through observations, the measures it has taken to comply with EU law.

6.2.2 Pre-litigation stage

6.2.2.1 The reasoned opinion by the Commission (Art. 258 TFEU)

The 'reasoned opinion' is the first official stage in the infringements proceeding.

If the Commission, after receiving the response from the member state, considers that the state continues to be in a situation of infringement of EU law or, in case there is no response from the member state, it may proceed with the formal pre-litigation procedure by delivering a reasoned opinion.

The reasoned opinion delivered to the member state is confidential, not legally binding,[100] and cannot be challenged.[101] The notification must set out the reasons of fact and law which, in the opinion of the Commission, have led the member state to fail to fulfil its obligations (and must contain only those objections of the Commission presented in the

---

[98] The opportunity offered to the state to make comments, is considered by the Court as an essential guarantee, without which the infringement procedure, by States, of their assumed obligations, would be unfounded (illegal). See *Commission des Communautés Européennes c / République italienne*, C-274/83.

[99] In those cases, the Commission automatically opens a procedure.

[100] The notification does not bind the member state concerned, and its legal effect is possible only in connection with an eventual notice of the CJEU.

[101] See Case 48/65, *Lutticke*.

formal letter), the measures that the Commission considers necessary to bring the failure to an end and a time-limit, within which it expects the matter to be rectified. In the absence of a Treaty provision about the time within which the member state must submit comments, the Court has noted that "the Commission shall give a reasonable time, ordinarily two months, but the time limit may vary depending on the complexity of the case, urgency, whether the state was already informed before the initiation of the procedure".

The member state is not held to answer the notification letter sent by the Commission. However, if the member state decides to answer the European Commission, it must include measures taken in order to comply with EU law. The deadline for the implementation of measures and for response to the Commission's requirements is two months, but it may be extended at the request of the member state concerned, by a maximum of three months, if legislative measures must be adopted to comply with the reasoned opinion. In case the member state does not conform to the notification, the Commission may take the case before the CJEU.[102]

The delivery of the reasoned opinion exhausts the administrative or pre-litigation stage. The Commission may then exercise its discretion in deciding whether to take proceedings before the CJEU. The discretion of the Commission to pursue an Art. 258 TFEU action before the CJEU must be taken in the context of its Art. 17 (1) TEU duty to take appropriate action to ensure that every breach is rectified.

The reasons for not proceeding with an Art. 258 TFEU action were expressed by Advocate General Roemer in Case 7/71, *Commission v. France*. These reasons include:

-   the possibility of reaching an amicable settlement if formal proceedings are delayed;
-   the effects of the violation of the State's obligations are relatively minor; and
-   the probability of the Union provision in question being amended in the near future.

---

[102] It should be noted that, the Commission could decide to proceed with the case and notify the Court even if in the case that the member state implements the necessary measures to comply with the EU law after the deadline established by the European Commission.

Moreover, if a member state, which has agreed to rectify a breach of its obligations, has been given insufficient time to comply with the Commission's reasoned opinion, the CJEU may dismiss an Art. 258 TFEU action on the grounds of inadequate time limits.

The statistics appear to indicate the success of the administrative and pre-litigation stages, especially since 2006. Indeed, between 2006 and 2010, a total of 7,024 formal notices were delivered by the Commission. The total number of reasoned opinions during this period amounted to 2,622 of which "only" 863 cases were referred to the CJEU (see Figure 16).[103]

Figure 16. Number of steps taken in infringement proceedings in each year (2006 and 2010)

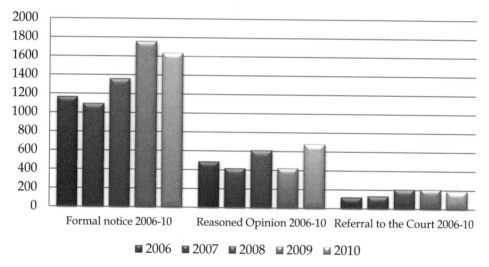

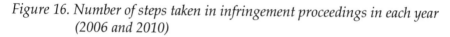

---

[103] There seems to be no rigorous empirical literature on the determinants of such infringements. That is, what fundamental factors or characteristics render it more likely that infringements occur? However, Guimaraes et al. (2010) have used a sample of 368 CJEU infringements cases on the free movement of goods in the period 1994-2002, in an attempt to explain country propensities to infringe by (institutional) country characteristics as well as by sectoral and trade characteristics. The authors show that infringements occur mainly in three sectors (food, beverages and tobacco; pharma and chemicals) and that. the higher regulatory quality in the EU country, the fewer the infringements. Nevertheless, we are cautious because the variables and data are subject to serious limitations.

6.2.2.2 *EU Pilot*

EU Pilot was launched in April 2008, following the European Commission adopted a Communication on "A Europe of Results – Applying Community Law".[104] The idea of the system is to provide quicker and better solutions to problems arising in the application of EU laws and quicker and better responses to inquiries for information, as well as to promote a less formal cooperation between the Commission and the member states. This method would help correct infringements of EU law at an early stage wherever possible, without the need for recourse to infringement proceedings. Indeed, since March 2010, the scope of EU Pilot has been expanded to cover all cases concerning the correct application and implementation of EU law and the conformity of the national law with EU law at an early stage before any possible recourse to an infringement procedure under Art. 258 TFEU.[105]

The EU Pilot project started operating with 15 member states participating on a voluntary basis, namely, Austria, Czech Republic, Denmark, Finland, Hungary, Ireland, Lithuania, the Netherlands, Portugal, Slovenia, Sweden, Spain and the United Kingdom. This first phase of the project is known as Pilot I.[106] Following the overall positive evaluation of first phase of the EU Pilot project (first evaluation report),[107] the Commission decided to continue to improve the project and the remaining 12 member states were invited to join. However, until today only ten additional member states have joined EU Pilot.[108] During this second phase of the EU Pilot project (Pilot II), which ran from April 2010 until September 2011, some improvements of the system have been introduced in order to

---

[104] See Communication from the Commission, "A Europe of Results – Applying Community Law", COM (2007) 502 final, Brussels, 5 September 2007.

[105] See Report from the Commission, "Second Evaluation Report on EU Pilot", SEC (2011) 1629/2, Brussels 21 December 2011.

[106] This initial phase of the EU Pilot project was evaluated by the Commission in its first EU Pilot Evaluation Report published in March 2010, which cover the period of the start-up of the project in April 2008 until March 2010. See Report from the Commission, "EU Pilot Evaluation Report", COM(2010) 70 final, Brussels, 3 March 2010.

[107] Ibid.

[108] Estonia and Slovakia (14.09.201), Bulgaria (14.10.2010), Belgium, Latvia, Poland and Romania (03.01.2011), Cyprus (07.03.2011), France and Greece (05.09.2011). Malta and Luxembourg have not yet joined EU Pilot.

promote its efficacy and efficiency. In effect, since 2010, EU Pilot has become a replacement of the informal phase of the infringement procedures whereby the Commission sent administrative letters to national administrations. It is a first step to infringement procedures.[109] However, where urgency or another overriding interest requires, the Commission can still immediately respond to an alleged infringement by a member state, without previous contacts through EU Pilot.[110] Taking into account the success of the system in increasing compliance with EU law and reducing the number of the infringement procedures, the Commission is now considering the possibility of extending EU Pilot as an instrument for problem-solving and prevention to all member states.[111]

Indeed, since the system was launched in April 2008 until September 2011, a total of 2,121 files were submitted to EU Pilot.[112] Of these, 1,410 files completed the process in EU Pilot. Furthermore, of the 4,035 cases entered into CHAP (the Commission's complaints handling system) in 2010, 686 complaints were sent for further attention to EU Pilot. However, it should be noted that the volume is not spread equally across all member states (as shown in Figure 17 below). Usually, there is a correlation between the population of the member states and the number of files received in EU Pilot. Moreover, there is a difference between the volume of files of those member states using the system since the start in 2008, and the others that joined the system later. Out of 2,121 files, 15.5% of them were submitted for Italy and Spain, 8% to the UK, 7.7% for Germany and 6.5% for Portugal.

---

[109] EU Pilot does not work as a mere alternative to the infringement proceedings, but rather as a complementary system, whilst still leaving room for infringement proceedings if unsuccessful.

[110] It should be noted, however, that the EU Pilot is an informal system and has no binding effect. This means that if a member state is unwilling to cooperate in this informal network, they have the right to do so. Furthermore, since it is an informal procedure, it should not be used while formal proceedings are already underway. Nevertheless, according to the principle of sincere cooperation, as laid down in Art. 4(3) TEU, the member states have to take any appropriate measure to fulfil the obligations arising out of the treaties or resulting from acts of the Union institutions. Cooperation in mechanisms such as EU Pilot can been seen as one such appropriate measure.

[111] Ibid.

[112] All the statistics on EU Pilot cited in this book cover the period 14 April 2008, when the system was launched, to 9 September 2011.

Figure 17. Volume of files – Breakdown by member state, 14 April 2008 to 9 September 2011

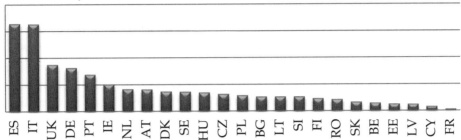

■ Number of files by member state

Source: Staff Working Paper, "Functioning of the system", accompanying the document Report from the Commission Second Evaluation Report on EU Pilot [SEC(2011) 1629/2), Brussels, 21 December 2011.

Member states refused to process only 2% of all submitted files in EU Pilot, the main reason being insufficient information transmitted by a complainant. With regard to the origin of files submitted to EU Pilot, 44% of the files are opened at the own initiative of the Commission, while 49% of the files are complaints and 7% of the files are requests for information sent by citizens or businesses. The files relate to a broad range issues: 33% concern environmental issues, 15% internal market, 10.5% taxation, 8% mobility and transport and 6% health and consumer protection (Figure 18).

Figure 18. Volume of files – Breakdown by Commission services, April 2008 to September 2011 (total files = 2121)

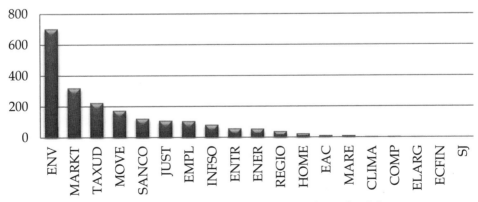

■ Volume of files submited - Breakdown by DG

Source: Staff Working Paper, "Functioning of the system", accompanying the document Report from the Commission Second Evaluation Report on EU Pilot, [SEC(2011) 1629/2), Brussels 21 December 2011.

The system works as follows. After receiving a complaint from a citizen or a business or by its own initiative,[113] the Commission will examine the complaint or enquiry, enter the issue and all the information received in the Pilot database and, subsequently, forward it to the EU Pilot Central Contact Point of the member state concerned.[114] The complaint will be accompanied by questions identified by the Commission.[115] Once entered into the EU Pilot database, the member state has 10 weeks in which to send a reply,[116] preferably providing a solution to identified problems.[117] From the start of EU Pilot in April 2008 and until 9 September 2011, the average time taken by member states for proposing a response to the Commission is 67 days, which is in line with the 10 weeks fixed for member states' responses (see Figure 19 below).

Having received the proposed solution by the member state, the Commission has 10 weeks[118] to evaluate whether the proposed solution is in conformity with EU law and the assessment of the member state's response is uploaded into the EU Pilot database. Since March 2008, the average time taken by the Commission services to assess the replies proposed by the member states' authorities and to decide on a follow-up of

---

[113] These include issues raised with the Commission in the European Parliament Petitions' Committee or via a letter from a Member of the European Parliament.

[114] The member state's EU Pilot Central Contact Point is usually part of the State's Ministry of Foreign Affairs, or another government office that occupies itself with European affairs.

[115] The issue, especially when based upon a complaint received from an individual or business, often needs to be rephrased to clearly identify the problem. To clarify the issue or to receive a satisfactory answer or solution, the Commission will ask for more information or even more directly for a proposed solution to the identified problem.

[116] This period of 10 weeks could be extended by the Commission at the request of the member state wherever justified. The decision is taken on a case-by case basis. Moreover, in exceptional cases, the Commission could decide to shorten the timeframe. However, in those cases, the Commission must explain to the member state the reason for its decision.

[117] That is much faster than the traditional procedure.

[118] It is important to note that the benchmark for the Commission has only been introduced with the adoption by the Commission of its first evaluation report on EU Pilot [COM (2010)70 final] on 3 March 2010.

the file is 102 days, which exceeds the general benchmark.[119] It should be noted that the credibility of the EU Pilot project depends on the speed of the whole process. Indeed, EU Pilot will be a credible pre-infringement procedure only if it will be able to solve the problems faced by citizens and business concerning the conformity of national law with EU law or the correct application of EU law, in an effective, efficient and rapid way.

Figure 19. The standard 10-week benchmark for member states (14 April 2008 to 9 September 2011)

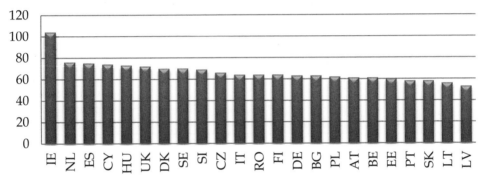

■ Number of average days elapsed between the submission of the file and proposal of a response by the member state concerned - Breakdown by member state

Source: Staff Working Paper, "Functioning of the system", accompanying the document Report from the Commission Second Evaluation Report on EU Pilot, [SEC(2011) 1629/2], Brussels 21 December 2011.

If the Commission decides to accept the position expressed by the member state, then the complainant is informed by the Commission of the action taken, and if the complainant does not object or complain in a period of four weeks, the case will be closed. In the event that the Commission is not satisfied with the solution provided by the member state, it can ask for more information, inform the member state that further action needs to be taken or, if an infringement is detected, the Commission may decide to launch an infringement procedure.[120] Of the 1,410 files processed in the

---

[119] It is to be noted that cases that exceed the benchmark are, for the most part, those where Commission services require additional information from national authorities, especially in the case of more complex files and those where translations are needed.

[120] If urgency is required, the Commission may decide to launch an infringement procedure right away, without going through the steps in EU Pilot.

system, nearly 80% (1,107 files) of the responses provided by the member states were assessed as acceptable, enabling the file to be closed without the need to launch an infringement procedure. The remaining 20% of the files (303) in which no acceptable solution in line with EU law could be found, went on to the infringement phase (see Table 5 below). Compared with the first evaluation report on EU Pilot, there was a decrease in the success rate (85% in 2010), mainly due to the increasing number of files opened after the new member states started to use EU Pilot.

Table 5. Success rate: Number of responses provided by member states assessed by the Commission services - Breakdown by DG - 14/04/2008 - 09/09/2011

DG	No. of responses	Opening infringement file	Accepted/rejected	Percentage of files with no need to open a formal infringement procedure = success rate
ENV	443	57	386	87.1%
SANCO	91	18	73	80.2%
TAXUD	147	55	92	62.6%
ENTR	55	13	42	76.4%
EMPL	73	26	47	64.4%
MARKT	247	62	185	74.9%
AGRI	43	0	43	100%
INFSO	47	7	40	85.1%
JUST	61	14	47	77%
REGIO	20	0	20	100%
ENER	41	4	37	90.2%
EAC	11	2	9	81.8%
HOME	14	4	10	71.4%
MOVE	113	41	72	63.7%
MARE	3	0	3	100%
COMP	1	0	1	100%
TOTAL	1,410	303	1,107	78.5%

Source: Staff Working Paper, "Functioning of the system", accompanying the document Report from the Commission Second Evaluation Report on EU Pilot, [SEC(2011) 1629/2], Brussels, 21 December 2011.

Since 2010, the Commission has observed a reduction in the volume of new infringement proceedings (adoption of a letter of formal notice under Art. 258 TFEU) (see Table 5). This reduction was greater in the original 15 member states that volunteered to join the EU Pilot project (Table 5). Furthermore, it should be noted that, since the adoption of the first report, EU Pilot must be used in all cases where additional factual or legal information is required for a full understanding of an issue at stake concerning the correct application, implementation of EU law or the conformity of the national law with EU law. Previously, the recourse to EU Pilot before initiating an infringement procedure was optional. This could explain why the reduction of infringement procedures is even more pronounced when comparing the data of 2009 with the data of 2011 (see Table 6 below).

Table 6. Evolution in the number of infringement procedures launched, 2009, 2010 and 2011 (reference year = 2009)

	2009	2010	2011*
Number of procedures launched	536	296	206
Change in number from 2009	–	-240	-330
Change in % from 2009	–	45%	42%

* Data for first nine months only.

Source: Staff Working Paper, "Functioning of the system", accompanying the document Report from the Commission Second Evaluation Report on EU Pilot, [SEC(2011) 1629/2], Brussels, 21 December 2011.

Even if it is not possible to identify all the reasons for this trend, one possible explanation is that EU Pilot helps to clarify and satisfactorily solve some issues regarding the application of EU law, without the need for recourse to infringement procedures and providing more rapid results for citizens and businesses. However, we should note that the increase in the number of cases submitted to EU Pilot has not yet led to a parallel decrease in the number of infringement procedures. Since its beginning until September 2011, 1,410 cases have been entered into the system. Although over 2009-11, the number of infringement procedures declined by only 330 files. This could mean that EU Pilot has contributed to a higher detection rate of non-compliance with EU law, by bringing to the system's attention cases that would not often lead to infringement procedures.

In sum, during the three-and-a-half-year period since EU Pilot was launched until September 2011, we conclude that the system has contributed to increased compliance with EU law, namely by solving different types of cases before they could turn into infringement cases and also by reducing the number of the infringement procedures.

6.2.3 Judicial stage

6.2.3.1 The referral to the Court of Justice of the EU (Art. 258 TFEU)

Referral to the Court of Justice of the European Union (CJEU) is the last means by which the Commission can pursue cases of persistent non-compliance of EU law. The appeal for finding the infringement of obligations assumed must be introduced, at the latest, within one month after the Commission decides to refer the case to the CJEU. However, before bringing the case, the Commission usually attempts to find some last-minute solution in bilateral negotiations with the member state.

Once the case is referred to the CJEU, the Commission is not able to add any other claims than those contained in the reasoned notification, but it can withdraw some of them. This means that new violations cannot be raised by the Commission in the proceedings before the CJEU.

The CJEU verifies whether the member state actually violated European law, as claimed by the Commission, and whether the measures demanded by the Commission are appropriate. Finally, the Court takes a decision.

The decision of the CJEU for failure to fulfil obligations assumed by member states is just a declaration. It establishes only the fact of an infringement and national authorities must then take measures in order to enforce the decision. The Court has no power to suspend or annul the state actions contested by the finding of EU law infringement or to execute concrete measures that the respondent State ought to take. The Court decision requires the State concerned to amend the legislation, adjusting it properly and, without delay, to adopt the measures ordered.

Although the Court decision only has effect between the parties, individuals can invoke the EU regulation, whose purpose and scope have been defined by the Court.

Within one month after the decision of the Court, the Commission sends a letter to the member state reminding it of the obligation to take necessary measures ensuring compliance with the EU law and to report, within three months, the measures taken or to be taken. The member state is expected to transmit a response to the Commission on the measures it has taken to comply with the decision of the Court.

If, following the transmission of observations by the member state concerned, the Commission still considers that the former has not taken the necessary measures to comply with the decision of the Court, it will issue a reasoned notification specifying the aspects on which the State has not complied with the decision of the Court.

6.2.3.2 Post-litigation infringement proceedings (Art. 260 TFEU)

If the member state refuses to comply with the CJEU judgment, the Commission may open new proceedings for post-litigation non-compliance, according to Art. 260 TFEU.

Prior to amendments made in the Maastricht Treaty, the only remedy under Art. 260 TFEU was a declaration by the CJEU that the member state had violated its obligations and that it should take the necessary steps to comply with the judgments of the Court. Nowadays, however, where the CJEU has found that the member state has failed to fulfil its obligations under the treaties, the member state is required to take the necessary measures to comply with the judgment of the CJEU. In short, it means that the Commission is empowered to specify the amount of the lump sum or penalty payment to be paid by the member state concerned, which it considers appropriate in the circumstances (Art. 260 (2) TFEU). In other words, if the concerned member state does not abide by the first decision of the CJEU (the first action establishes liability), the Commission can bring a new action to the CJEU (second action), requiring the CJEU to impose financial penalties, either in the form of a lump sum or a daily fine, calculated by taking into account the scope and duration of the infringement as well as the capabilities of the member state concerned, the effect of the infringement on the public and private interest and the urgency of the matter.[121] The fines, which are imposed by the CJEU, result from this second action brought before the CJEU by the Commission and

---

[121] Art. 260 TFEU contains no guidance on the limits of the fines or penalties nor on how they are to be enforced. However, according to the case law of the CJEU (see Cases C-387/97, *Commission v. Greece* and C-304/02, *Commission v. France*), the criteria to be taken into account to ensure that the penalty payments have coercive force and that European law would be applied uniformly and effectively are:
-   the duration of the infringement,
-   its degree of seriousness and
-   the ability of the member state to pay the penalty.

not from the first one, which only establishes the liability of the member state.

Indeed, according to Art. 260, section 2, paragraph 3 of the TFEU, the infringement by the member state of the Court decision constitutes a new violation of the Treaty provisions which may be sanctioned again with an action of obligations infringement.

Moreover, there is no requirement for a reasoned opinion to be delivered prior to a second court case being brought by the Commission.

7. ENFORCEMENT BARRIERS IN INTRA-EU CROSS-BORDER PUBLIC PROCUREMENT

7.1 Factors influencing cross-border procurement tenders and awards

The market value of public procurement in the EU-27 is enormous, representing some 16% of GDP. However, when focusing on intra-EU cross-border procurement, it is far less, although still impressive: some €420 billion (about 3.6% of EU GDP) in 2009 was published in the EU's Tender Electronic Daily (TED), as required when the purchase is above the relevant threshold value. Not all of these contracts relate to goods (supplies): they also include services as well as public (infrastructural) works as such. Companies are typically reluctant to tender cross-border, even inside the EU (or EEA). There are many reasons for this reluctance and it is therefore inappropriate to blame protectionism or (illicit) barriers thrown up by other member states or their regions or other procuring authorities. Such attitudes may well linger and some such 'barriers' might still escape scrutiny despite extensive EU legislation as well as national and EU appeal procedures, but there are many other reasons that should be kept in mind. Figure 20 gives eight reasons from a recent survey.

Reasons such as "no experience doing business abroad", "too much local competition" and "language barriers" all score high and have, of course, nothing to do with (enforcement or internal market) barriers. Of the other motives, "legal barriers" might well rest on perceptions because EU rules have existed for a long time now and numerous cases as well as often-used complaint procedures (nowadays in EU Pilot, and nationally, see below) surely have reduced such "legal barriers" significantly. Unless companies mean something else, namely, that the considerable leeway for member states to build on the minimum common provisions of the basic procurement directives with a range of procedural and substantive details, which is allowed by these 'coordination' directives, as we shall explain. This national discretion may cause procedures, requirements and substance to differ more than desirable between the 27 EU countries, resulting in (costly) regulatory heterogeneity. Such regulatory heterogeneity is regarded by companies interested in EU-wide (or, at least, intra-EU cross-border) business as a 'barrier', a cost-increasing feature of cross-border procurement tenders. Thus, this aspect may well overlap with another motive given, "higher costs", as well as with "more resources to tender" and possibly with "administrative requirements" (larger than at home).

Figure 20. Reasons for not bidding cross-border

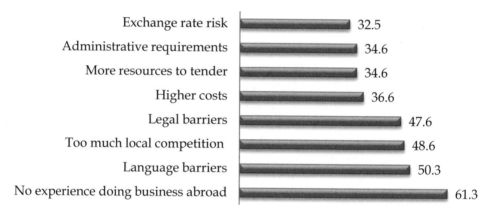

Source: European Commission, "EU public procurement legislation: delivering results, summary of evaluation report", 2011.

There is a host of other factors influencing the propensity to bid and difficulties to overcome before being successful in obtaining awards. One is that member states exhibit a great variation in the degree of (de)centralisation in procurement, with an estimated total of some 250,000 contracting authorities in the EU. In France alone, there are several tens of thousands of purchasing authorities (with some 300,000 public officials working on bids and awards). Whereas (in 2006-09) Finland procures some 50% of contract value locally, Portugal, Estonia, Slovakia, Bulgaria and Cyprus have local shares of 10% or less, that is, they mainly purchase centrally. Contracts from utilities assume a very small share in Slovenia and the Netherlands, whereas they make up one-third or more in e.g. Austria, Belgium, Greece and Hungary. A second factor is the sectoral composition: in the one-fifth of total public procurement in the EU that is published in the TED, there is almost no tender for supply of goods and services to health, education and social services, which are typically local and these sectors are not covered – despite the fact that they form roughly 6% of the 16% of GDP. A third reason is the relative difficulty for SMEs to obtain contracts. Between 2006 and 2008, SMEs took 60% of the contracts directly making up 34% of the total value; another 8% were obtained indirectly via subcontracting. Still, the 66% remaining of direct contract value was acquired by a relatively few large firms.

All these aspects are possible factors other than 'barriers' that might hinder the acquisition of cross-border contracts for certain firms. Against this backdrop, implementation and enforcement 'barriers' in cross-border public procurement can be analysed. Before doing so, a brief summary of EU public procurement legislation is provided.

7.2 How the EU disciplines national and regional public procurement

In the EU internal market, national, regional and local public procurement as well as procurement of state-owned enterprises not subject to competitive markets should be open, transparent, non-discriminatory and competitive. These are the aims of EU public procurement legislation ever since the 1970s. But this is easier said than done. If one wishes to beat the ingenuity of protectionist officials, or the politicians 'behind' them, one quickly finds that numerous details have to be regulated or restricted and extensive reporting requirements are needed. The upshot is an enormous bureaucracy for public bodies and a lot of red tape for business. A loose regime, on the other hand, is likely to be misused, even though competitive procurement is cutting costs and promoting quality for national and sub-national governments.

Moreover, with too many detailed rules and easy litigation or appeals, national officials also become overly prudent, that is, in order to be 'safe', public procurement deteriorates into 'ticking off items' on a long list of bureaucratic requirements instead of focusing on obtaining 'value for money'. Value-for-money refers to an appropriate combination of quality of the goods or services and low costs. At times, this may also refer to a wider, public-policy driven perspective of 'quality' in pursuing some other objectives like promoting innovation, stimulating SMEs, promoting social inclusion, environmental protection (via 'green' procurement) and promoting 'fair' trade (e.g. for farmers in developing countries). EU public procurement law finds itself in a permanent struggle to address this trade-off between less red tape and 'better' public procurement, on the one hand,

and the pursuit of an open, competitive internal public procurement market, on the other. Recent proposals by the Commission represent a new attempt to address these challenges.

The first procurement directives were adopted in the 1970s to regulate bids and contracts for works and supplies for public bodies. Since then they have been extended and amended many times. At present, the rules on contract award procedures are, mainly, contained in two directives adopted in 2004:

- Directive 2004/18/EC[122] (the so-called public sector Directive or classic Directive). This regulates tender bids and contracts awarded by public bodies, in particular of supplies of goods and services and some public works; and

- Directive 2004/17/EC[123] (the so-called utilities Directive), which regulates procurement in four specific areas of activity, namely water, energy, transport and postal service.[124]

The directives are only concerned with the creation of an internal market in public procurement. They are not intended to provide a general system for pursuing objectives found in national procurement systems, such as ensuring best value for taxpayers' money. Moreover, they only apply to contracts above a certain financial value (thresholds). The justification of thresholds consists of two basic arguments: i) only a minimum value of turnover will be able to attract suppliers from other

---

[122] Directive 2004/18/EC of the European Parliament and of the Council of 31 March 2004 on the coordination of procedures for the award of public works contracts, public supply contracts and public services contracts.

[123] Directive 2004/17/EC of the European Parliament and of the Council of 31 March 2004 coordinating the procurement procedures of entities operating in the water, energy, transport and postal services sectors.

[124] Apart from those two main directives, there are two directives concerning the legal protection of bidders participating in public procurement procedures (Directives 89/665/EEC and 92/13/EEC, modified by Directive 2007/66/EC of the European Parliament and of the Council of 11 December 2007 amending Council Directives 89/665/EEC and 92/13/EEC with regard to improving the effectiveness of review procedures concerning the award of public contracts) and a special Directive for defence and sensitive procurement (Directive 2009/81/EC on the coordination of procedures for the award of certain works contracts, supply contracts and service contracts by contracting authorities or entities in the fields of defence and security, and amending Directives 2004/17/EC and 2004/18/EC).

member states, given the expected efforts to submit a competitive tender bid; and ii) the red tape for EU-wide competitive procurement is costly, both for governments and for companies and it makes sense to operate within a reasonable cost-benefit framework.[125] The current thresholds are nevertheless often criticised as being too low, certainly in the case of supplies. The problem here is that, apart from cost-benefit considerations, the chances for SMEs to compete decline with the increasing size of contracts.

The directives do not lay down an exhaustive set of procurement rules; they leave room for member states' own rules, provided that these rules are consistent with the directives. This means, for example, that member states may adopt stricter rules than those in the directives.

The public sector Directive applies to all types of procurement contracts (works contracts, supply contracts and services contracts). However, the Directive does not apply fully to all services contracts. These are divided into priority services, which are subject to the Directive's full rules, and non-priority services, which are subject only to the Directive's rules on technical specifications, award notices and statistics (also called A-services and B-services, respectively). The priority services are listed in Annex IIA (e.g. IT services, consultancy and accountancy), and they have been selected on the basis of their potential scope for cross-border trade, potential savings and the availability of information on the services.

---

[125] A Europe Economics (2006) study estimated enforcement and compliance costs for authorities at some 0.7% of contract value on average. In European Commission (2011, ch. 8), the overall figure is around 1.3% of value, covering all costs during the entire process, including litigation if any. The reader should note that the average conceals a huge variety in contract values. This amounts to an average of €28,000 procedure costs for all involved, one-fifth for the authorities (€5,500 per call for tender) and €3,800 per tendering firm, times the average number of firms putting in a bid, which is 5.9. The estimated savings on average for above-threshold contracts is about 5%, to be set against 1.3% average costs. However, the lower the contract value, the higher the share of costs: at the lowest threshold (€125,000), such costs for all involved may add up to between 18% and 29% (again, to be divided between authorities and the number of bidders). This underpins the often-heard insistence to increase the thresholds for simple supply contracts. The reader is reminded that most of such costs would be incurred anyway, also without EU rules. In European Commission, 2011, the additional costs of compliance with EU directives as compared to below-threshold contracts is found to be about 0.2% for authorities and another 0.2% for suppliers.

Although coverage is broad, some contracts are excluded from the scope of the Directive.[126] However, some member states have opted for extending the Directive to areas not covered or only partially covered by the directives. For example, some member states have extended the Directive to concessions, to annex B services, to social services or to contracts below the thresholds of the Directive. Indeed, many of the annual 150,000 notifications in TED are below-threshold contracts.

The public sector Directive, as mentioned above, only applies to contracts above certain thresholds (Arts 7 to 9) (these values are indicated in Table 7 below). In order to prevent purchasers from splitting contracts into smaller amounts, so as to bring them below the regulatory thresholds and, consequently, fall outside the scope of the Directive, it includes two sets of provisions. First, such practices are forbidden (Art. 9 (3)) and, second, a purchaser is held to add together the value of purchases made under similar contracts (aggregation rule) and the Directive will apply if the total value of those contracts exceeds the threshold. The aggregation rule helps to prevent purchasers from evading the rules and provides an incentive for authorities to award a single contract that might attract cross-border competition, although it risks making it more difficult for SMEs to participate.

---

[126] The main exclusions are the services concession contracts, certain contracts awarded to another contracting authority, some contracts for hard defence equipment and other contracts affected by various concerns relating to secrecy and security, contracts governed by different procedural rules connected with joint projects with non-member states, those by international bodies (e.g. the United Nations or the World Bank) and those made pursuant to international agreements on the stationing of troops. Contracts on arbitration or conciliation services, certain financial services contracts, some research contracts and development services contracts, the utility contracts regulated in the utilities Directive and contracts in the sector of telecommunications activities, which were previously regulated by the utilities Directive (but now excluded from its scope, given the liberalisation of telecommunications) are excluded as well from the scope of the public sector Directive (Arts 12 to 17 of the Directive). The authorities can also dispense from some of the usual rules, where necessary and to the extent necessary, award contracts for the design and construction of public housing schemes (Art. 34).

Table 7. Thresholds specified in Directive 2004/18/EC from 1 January 2012

Central government authorities	Works contracts, works concessions contracts, subsidised works contracts		€5 million
	All contracts concerning services listed in Annex II B, certain telecommunication services and R&D services; all design contests concerning these services and all subsidised services		€200,000
	All contracts and design contests concerning services listed in Annex II A except contracts and design contests concerning certain telecommunication services and R&D services		€130,000
	A supplies contracts awarded by contracting authorities **not** operating in the field of defence		€130,000
	Supplies contracts awarded by contracting authorities operating in the **field of defence**	Concerning products listed in Annex V	€130,000
		Concerning other products	€200,000
Sub-central contracting authorities	Works contracts, works concessions contracts, subsidised works contracts		€5 million
	All service contracts, all design contests, subsidised service contracts, all supplies contracts		€200,000

The utilities Directive regulates procurement by entities operating in four sectors: water, energy, transport and postal services.[127] Art. 30 of the Directive provides that it does not apply to an activity "directly exposed to competition on markets to which access is not restricted". The exemption only applies when the Commission takes a positive formal decision that the conditions for an exemption exist.[128] This possibility has been provided for in the implementing legislation of the majority of member states, except Belgium, Denmark, Estonia, France, Latvia and Poland. By June 2011, 25 applications had been received by the Commission for 10 member states, concerning the postal and energy sectors. Three of these requests were withdrawn and 18 decisions were adopted. The 18 decisions relate to nine

---

[127] Previously, the Directive regulated telecommunication services, but this sector was omitted from the 2004 Directive as a result of the liberalisation of the sector.

[128] The detailed procedures for making exemption decisions are set out in Commission Decision 2005/15/EC of 7 January 2005.

different member states and 11 of these decisions were positive, four mixed and three negative.

The rules on contracts covered by the utilities Directive are similar to those of the public sector Directive. The most important differences are higher threshold values for supply and services contracts (works contracts: €5 million; all supplies and services, all design contests: €400,000)[129] and a number of additional exemptions.

Under the public sector Directive, contracting authorities must use one of five types of award procedures: open procedure, restricted procedure, competitive dialogue, negotiated procedure with a contract notice and negotiated procedure without notice. As a general rule, authorities must use either the open procedure or the restricted procedure (Art. 28); the other ones, which are considered less transparent, are available only in special cases. The contracts, with limited exceptions (e.g. negotiated procedure without a notice)[130] must be advertised in the TED series of the EU's Official Journal (a contract notice). The key information from the notice is published in all EU languages. The Commission has developed search tools that are available on the Commission's SIMAP website, which also include links to national websites offering advertisements for contracts below the thresholds.

The utilities Directive provides more flexible procedural rules than the public sector Directive. This is explained by the complexity of such contracts and the duration and management of infrastructural works. Under the utilities Directive, authorities may choose the negotiated procedure with a notice, as well as the open or restricted procedure, for any contract. Moreover, the utilities Directive, in addition to the advertisement of the contract through a contract notice, requires the following:

- Advertisement through a periodic indicative notice (PIN). This is an advance notice of general requirements for the year and can be used to advertise specific contracts as long as such specific contracts are referred to in the PIN.
- Advertising a qualification system, in fact, a list on which firms interested in particular types of contracts can be registered (if they qualify). Individual contracts can be awarded simply by inviting firms on the list, without further advertisement.

---

[129] Values from 1 January 2012 onwards.

[130] This procedure is only available for cases specified in Art. 31 of the Directive.

7.3 Implementation and application of EU public procurement law

When it comes to implementation and application problems in public procurement (that is, what one may call 'enforcement barriers' in the internal market), the picture is not so encouraging. Having said this, it is also true that correction mechanisms are built into the system, both at national and EU level and they do help, if only after considerable delays. Moreover, one should not forget that no less than 150,000 notifications of (TED) tenders are made annually, a huge number, so that the frictions and problems in the system have to be seen in this light. In the following section, we shall first deal briefly with implementation problems between 2005 and 2010, subsequently with EU enforcement efforts following complaints to the Commission and finally with the considerable national review and remedies systems (operating under Directive 2007/66/EC).

The implementation process of the utilities Directive and the public sector Directive, adopted 31 March 2004, with a deadline for transposition into the national legislation of 31 January 2006 for all member states,[131] was problematic, to say the least. Only seven member states implemented the public sector Directive on time. Thus, in March 2006, the European Commission opened 18 infringement procedures for non-transposition of the public sector Directive. The last country to transpose the Directive was Belgium in 2010 (Table 8 below).

Six infringement procedures concerning non-conformity of national rules implementing the Directive with certain of its provisions were not yet closed in April 2011.[132]

The transposition of the utilities Directive was also delayed in 16 member states, which resulted in the launch of 16 infringement procedures for non-transposition. Today the Directive has been fully transposed by all the member states (see Table 9). Several infringement procedures were also open for non-conformity of national rules with specific provisions of the Directive. Two of these cases were still pending in April 2011.[133]

---

[131] Romania and Bulgaria were required to implement the directives by the date of their accession to the European Union, 1 January 2007.

[132] According to the Commission Evaluation Report on the Impact and Effectiveness of EU Public Procurement Legislation, published in 27.06.2011, SEC(2011) 853 final.

[133] Ibid.

Table 8. Overview of national implementation of Directive 2004/18/EC

2004/18/EC				
Member state	Procedure opened	Closed	Comments	Implemented by
BE	03.2006	03.2010	Judgment	09.2009
BG		–		01.2007
CZ	03.2006	10.2006		07.2006
DK				01.2005
DE	03.2006	12.2006		11.2006
EE	03.2006	03.2007		05.2007
IE	03.2006	10.2006		06.2006
EL	03.2006	06.2007	Referral decided	03.2007
ES	03.2006	12.2007	Referral executed	10.2007
FR	03.2006	10.2006		08.2006
IT	03.2006	10.2006		07.2006
CY				02.2006
LV	03.2006	12.2006		05.2006
LT	03.2006	10.2006		07.2006
LU	03.2006	10.2009	Judgment	08.2009
HU	03.2006	12.2006		10.2006
MT		–		06.2006
NL		–		01.2006
AT		–		01.2007
PL	03.2006	10.2006		05.2006
PT	03.2006	09.2008	Referral decided	07.2008
RO		–		02.2007
SL	03.2006	06.2007		03.2007
SK		–		02.2006
FI	03.2006	06.2007	Referral decided	06.2007
SE	03.2006	04.2008	Judgment	01.2008
UK		–		01.2006

Source: European Commission, "Evaluation Report on the Impact and Effectiveness of EU Public Procurement Legislation", SEC (2011) 853, of 27.06.2011.

Table 9. Overview of national implementation of the Directive 2004/17/EC

2004/17/EC				
Member State	Procedure opened	Closed	Comments	Implemented by
BE	03.2006	03.2010	Judgment	02.2010
BG				01.2007
CZ	03.2006	10.2006		07.2006
DK				01.2005
DE	03.2006	12.2006		11.2006
EE	03.2006	03.2007		05.2007
IE	03.2006	03.2007		03.2007
EL	03.2006	06.2007	Referral decided	03.2007
ES	03.2006	12.2007	Referral executed	10.2007
FR	03.2006	12.2006		08.2006
IT	03.2006	10.2006		07.2006
CY		–		02.2006
LV		–		12.2004
LT	03.2006	10.2006		07.2006
LU	03.2006	10.2009	Judgment	08.2009
HU		–		05.2004
MT		–		06.2005
NL		–		01.2006
AT		–		02.2006
PL	03.2006	10.2006		05.2006
PT	03.2006	09.2008	Judgment	07.2008
RO		–		02.2007
SL	03.2006	06.2007		03.2007
SK		–		02.2006
FI	03.2006	06.2007	Referral decided	06.2007
SE	03.2006	04.2008	Judgment	01.2008
UK		–		01-2006

Source: European Commission, "Evaluation Report on the Impact and Effectiveness of EU Public Procurement Legislation", SEC (2011) 853, of 27.06.2011.

EU enforcement of public procurement at national level concerns, in the final analysis, the infringement of EU law. It should be realised that the national review and remedies procedures, to be discussed later, have a different purpose: of course, compliance with EU law may be an issue but the aim of review and remedies in member states is to respect the proper treatment and individual rights of bidders in any specific national contract award. In other words, it is protecting bidders from mistakes and possible tricks by correcting such improper conduct via national bodies specially established for this purpose.

EU enforcement of public procurement, already difficult because of the sheer magnitude of the market, is made more cumbersome by the nature of the EU directives. The public sector Directive and the utilities Directive are 'coordination' directives, which do not harmonise public procurement rules in detail. This means that the member states are allowed to go beyond the minimum requirements set in the directives. Many member states have used this possibility to supplement the minimum requirements of the procurement Directive in national legislation. The result is a *fragmentation* in national legislation on public procurement, according to sectors, levels of governance and the number of different acts applicable to public procurement. This may create difficulties for both contracting authorities and bidders in identifying the applicable rules. Furthermore, many member states have introduced additional provisions clarifying EU provisions, in an attempt to reduce legal uncertainty and encourage non-discriminatory competition, by means of transparency requirements, more legal protection of third parties, additional obligations for publicity or conditions that the tender participants have to meet. Such regulatory heterogeneity, with respect to national regulatory autonomy, can be costly from a business point of view.

In 2010, the European Commission received 226 new complaints in the area of public procurement. The countries most concerned were Germany, Italy, Greece, the UK and Bulgaria.

Enquiries and complaints in the field of public procurement have been increasingly treated within the new EU Pilot system since its introduction in April 2008. Indeed, there is a significantly higher use of EU Pilot in procurement than in other areas. Public procurement EU Pilot cases accounted for around 50% of all cases in the internal market and services from 2008 until 2010 (50% in 2010, 43% in 2009 and 50% in 2008), and the system has been used in a very proactive way, resulting in 90% of the EU Pilot cases being closed in 2009.

Figure 21. Number of files handled by the European Commission in the field of public procurement, 2007-10

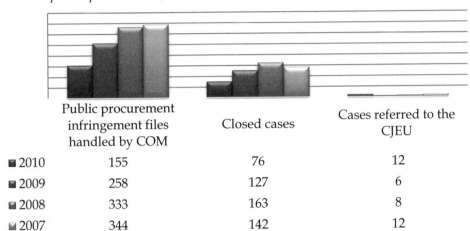

	Public procurement infringement files handled by COM	Closed cases	Cases referred to the CJEU
2010	155	76	12
2009	258	127	6
2008	333	163	8
2007	344	142	12

Source: European Commission, Annual Reports on Monitoring the Application of EU Law.

As shown in Figure 21, the number of public procurement infringement files handled by the European Commission each year has progressively decreased in the period 2007-10 (155 in 2010, 258 in 2009, 333 in 2008 and 344 in 2007). Most of the files opened by the Commission were closed during the pre-administrative/administrative phase of the infringement procedure (76, 127, 163 and 142, respectively). However, in comparative terms, the number of cases referred to the Court of Justice of the European Union increased slightly in 2010 (7.5% of the cases in 2010 had been reported to the CJEU, compared with 2.3% of the cases in 2009, 2.4% in 2008 and 3.5% in 2007).

Even if the number of infringement procedures opened by the Commission in the reported period had decreased in relation to previous years, the case load of public procurement infringement complaints still remains high and indicates that compliance levels should be improved in a number of member states.

The European Commission's "Evaluation Report on the Impact and Effectiveness of EU Public Procurement Legislation",[134] based on a sample of 78 infringement procedures opened by the European Commission since

---

[134] SEC(2011) 853 final.

2005 and issued with a reasoned opinion and were not related to late transposition of the Directives, finds that the majority of the cases concerned the public sector Directive. Only nine cases were concerned with the utilities Directive and six other cases were concerned with both directives.

As expected, in a large majority of the cases (48 cases), a contract had been awarded without a previous award procedure with prior publication at EU level or, in some cases, at least without adequate publicity with respect to contracts not or not fully subjected to the detailed provisions of the directives. Four cases were related to problems in the negotiations, namely the choice of a negotiated procedure. The distinction between selection and award criteria posed problems in seven cases. Problems relating to regional and/or national preferences arose in seven cases. Other issues concerning the incorrect follow-up of CJEU judgements were raised in seven cases involving four member states whilst undue limitations for subcontracting and/or otherwise relying on the capacities of other economic operators were found in two cases.

7.4   The remedies Directive (2007/66/EC) - National review and the possibility of remedies for improper treatment of bidders

Procedures providing effective mechanisms to seek redress in cases where suppliers/bidders deem that the contract has been unfairly awarded are essential to establish trust and ensure the appropriate functioning of a procurement system. Indeed, when economic operators, for whatever reason, do not agree with decisions taken by public authorities in relation to a public procurement procedure, they can challenge those decisions by initiating a domestic review procedure that should comply with certain minimum requirements. Moreover, a public complaints review and remedies system serves as a deterrent to breaking the law and helps to correct violations of the law. Therefore, an effective functioning public procurement review and remedies system at the member state level may ultimately contribute to the achievement of the objectives of the substantive procurement rules, such as transparency, non-discrimination and equal treatment as well as 'value for money'.

The legal framework with regard to judicial protection in the area of public procurement consists of Directives 89/665/EEC (remedies Directive for public sector) and 92/13/EEC4 (remedies Directive for the utilities sector). The first directive coordinates the review procedures of the member states in connection with public sector contracts, while the second relates specifically to utility contracts. These two directives were substantially amended by Directive 2007/66/EC, which should have been transposed by the member states into national law by 20 December 2009.

The main objective of the public complaints review and remedies system is to enforce the correct practical application of public procurement legislation.

The remedies Directives stipulate that member states must take the necessary measures to ensure that decisions taken by contracting authorities may be reviewed effectively and, in particular, as rapidly as possible. They also refer to the principle of equivalence: there may be no discrimination between undertakings as a result of the distinction between national rules implementing EU law and other national rules. Review procedures should be available to any person having or having had an interest in obtaining a public contract. The member states are required to ensure that the authorities responsible for reviewing allegedly unlawful decisions have the power to take interim measures as soon as possible and in summary proceedings. In addition, they must have the power to set aside or ensure the setting aside of decisions taken unlawfully and to award damages.

First, the existing legal framework in the area of public procurement at the EU level will be set out, focusing on the two most important problems Directive 2007/66 is intended to solve: the race to contract signature and the illegal direct award of contracts.

With the new Directive 2007/66/EC, the Commission's aim is to resolve two main problems. The first one is that it should become easier in practice to ensure that the signing of a disputed contract could be prevented in time (this problem occurs in the pre-contractual phase).[135] This problem occurs when there is a desire on the part of a contracting authority to conclude the awarded contract very quickly after the award decision has been taken in order to make the consequences of that decision irreversible. This conduct makes it impossible for rejected competitors of the successful tender to start a review procedure in time to challenge an allegedly unlawful award decision, since once the contract has been concluded,

---

[135] Case C-81/89, *Alcatel Austria*. In its judgment, the CJEU clarified that review should be made possible by allowing for a reasonable period between the award decision and the conclusion of the contract. The possibility of obtaining damages alone was deemed insufficient by the Court.

rejected tenders only have the possibility to claim damages. However, obviously, an unsuccessful tender is not primarily interested in financial compensation, but in a challenge of the award decision so that in the end he can conclude and perform the contract himself instead of a competitor.

The second problem is related to illegal direct awards (i.e. contracts awarded without prior notification and competition in breach of the public procurement Directives).[136]

In order to prevent this from happening, Directive 2007/66/EC introduces two main features:

- **A standstill period.** Contracting authorities need to wait for at least 10 days after deciding who has won the public contract before the contract can actually be signed. This period gives bidders time to examine the decision and decide whether to initiate a review procedure. If they decide to do so within the standstill period, this results in the automatic suspension of the procurement process until the review body takes its decision. If it is proved that the rules had not been respected, the national bodies must render the signed contract ineffective.

- **More stringent rules against illegal direct awards of public contracts.** National courts are now able to render these contracts ineffective in the event that they have been illegally awarded without transparency and prior competitive tendering.

Moreover, for contracts based on framework agreements and a dynamic purchasing system, where speed and efficiency may be particularly relevant, the Directive provides for a specific review mechanism. In these types of contracts, member states may choose to replace the standstill obligation by a post-contractual review procedure.

Table 10 below summarises the available data on the number of review remedies in 22 member states. However, it should be noted that it is not possible to directly compare the numbers, since they refer to different years or refer to the cumulative number of both procedures above and below the EU threshold (e.g. Sweden) or to all cases submitted to the administrative courts (e.g. Luxembourg).

---

[136] Case C-26/03, Stadt Halle. The illegal direct award of public contracts has been classified by the CJEU as the case with "the most serious breach of Community law in the field of public procurement".

Table 10. Summary of review remedies in selected member states

Member state	No. of complaints	Comments
Bulgaria	1,103 complaints before the court; 799 rulings (2009)	Total number of public procurement contracts in 2009: 16,071
Czech Republic	459 complaints; 391 first instance ruling; 89 preliminary rulings (2009)	High deposits, loser-pays principle and reputational risks prevent the tenderers from filing complaints
Denmark	75 (2009); 181 (2010)	Risk to reputation prevents the tenderers from filing complaints
Germany	1,158 (court of first instance); 227 (court of second instance)	
Ireland	No numbers available	Clear preference for the dialogue method; bringing an action before the court viewed as last resort
Greece	No numbers available	Parties often challenge award decisions
France	5,000 before the court (2004)	
Italy		Around 40% of the case law in the Administrative Courts
Cyprus	No numbers available	Parties often challenge award decisions
Latvia	200 per year	High deposits and loser pays principle prevent the tenderers from filing complaints
Luxembourg	53 (2009)	
Hungary	636 (2008)	No. of procedures have decreased since 2005
Malta	No numbers available	High court and lawyer fees discourage complaints
Austria	106 review applications; 90 petitions; 8 declaratory procedures (2010)	High court fees discourage complaints

Poland	1,537 Appeals court; 227 second instance (2008)	Short period of review procedure
Portugal	No numbers available	High court and lawyer fees and lengthy procedures discourage complaints
Romania	6,607 (2008 and 2009)	Only one-third of complaints are admitted
Slovenia	No numbers available	High court fees discourage complaints
Slovakia	1,089 (2005)	High court and lawyer fees, lengthy procedures and risk to reputation discourage complaints
Finland	600 (2009)	
Sweden	3,154 (2010)	The figures are for both above and below threshold
United Kingdom	No numbers available	High lawyer fees and risk to reputation discourage complaints

Source: European Commission, "Evaluation Report, Impact and Effectiveness of EU Public Procurement Legislation", Staff Working Paper, Part 1, SEC(2011) 853 final.

From the table above, we can conclude that the legal costs associated with the action (court and lawyers fees) are the main reason inhibiting the filing of complaints by tenderers in many member states. This is true even for countries that are very active and innovative in the promotion of public procurement legislation (e.g. the UK). Lengthy legal procedures also discourage complaints. In small member states, the reputational risk plays also an important role as a disincentive to complain. By contrast in those countries where the associated cost of the legal proceeding is relatively low, we can observe an extensive recourse to the review procedures (e.g. Romania). Nevertheless, there is ample evidence of the significance of national review and remedies, with numerous bidders seeking review in many EU countries. These reviews may eventually help to reduce mistrust and remove more of the inhibitions to cross-border public procurement bids as well.

7.5   The European Commission's new legislative proposals

In December 2011, the European Commission – after an in-depth evaluation, an intensive process of consultation aimed at assessing the application and effects of EU public procurement in the past and the completion of several studies[137] – proposed three draft directives on public procurement.[138] These proposals are part of an overall programme aiming at an in-depth modernisation and simplification of public procurement in the European Union.

The proposed reform aims to simplify and make more flexible the existing rules and procedures, encourage access to public procurement for SMEs, facilitate a qualitative improvement in the use of public procurement and complete the legal European public procurement framework.

The main changes introduced by the new legislative proposals are the following:

-   **Extension of the regime to all services.** The new proposals abolish the previous distinction between A services and B services. The new rules will apply to all services, with the exception of 'social services'. Member states will be free to determine which procedural rules will be applicable to the procurement of social services. The only compulsory requirement is to publish the contract notice and the contract award notice in the Official Journal of the EU.

-   **Extension of the exclusion in the utilities Directive.** The European Commission is proposing to add the exploration of oil and gas to the existing exclusions under the utilities regime.

---

[137] http://ec.europa.eu/internal_market/publicprocurement/modernising_rules/consultations/index_en.htm.

[138] Proposal for a Directive of the European Parliament and of the Council on public procurement replacing Directive 2004/18/EC, COM(2011)0896 final, Proposal for a Directive of the European Parliament and of the Council on Procurement by entities operating in the water, energy, transport and postal services sectors replacing Directive 2004/17/EC, COM(2011)0895 final and Proposal for a Directive of the European Parliament and of the Council on the award of concession contracts, COM(2011)897 final.

- **In-house exemptions.** The revised rules set out the conditions under which procurement may benefit from the so-called 'Teckal in house exemption'.[139]

- **Introduction of new award procedure.** The 'competitive dialogue' procedure will no longer be restricted to complex cases. Moreover, two new procedures are introduced: the 'competitive procedure with negotiation' and the 'innovative partnership', given that the open and the restricted procedures are inappropriate for long-term, complex and high-value procurement contracts. The first procedure is similar to the existing negotiated procedure. The contracting entities could negotiate directly with the tenderers with the aim to improve the content of their offers. However, the description of the procurement, the minimum requirements defined in the technical specifications and the award criteria could not be changed in the course of the negotiations. The second new procedure is aimed at establishing a structured partnership for the development of an innovative product, service or works.

- **Simplification of the framework agreements, dynamic purchasing system, electronic auctions and electronic catalogues.** The objective is to support the use of electronic procurement procedures.

- **Simplification of the procurement regime for all sub-central contracting authorities.** In the public sector, when contracting with sub-central contracting authorities such as local authorities, it will be possible to use an OJEU prior information notice (PIN), in the case of restricted and competitive procedures with negotiation, instead of requiring an OJEU contract notice.

- **New rules for joint procurements by contracting entities.** The proposals introduce new rules on occasional joint procurement by contracting entities from the same or different member states.

- **Inclusion of the service concession contracts.** Presently the service concession contracts are the only concession not regulated at EU level. The proposed new rules are intended to apply to both public

---

[139] Laid down by the CJEU in July 1999 in *Teckal (C-107/98)*, the case established the rule that where a public body enters into a service contract with a body over which it exercises decisive control and which provides the essential part of its services back to the parent body, this contract is not subject to the procurement rules. This has been expanded in subsequent case law to cover services provided by 'shared service' bodies controlled collectively by public bodies.

sector and utilities concessions with a value equal to or greater than €5 million and are based upon the same rules that apply to public sector and utility procurement.

- **Award criteria.** Both proposals allow contracting authorities to award a contract based only on the "most economically advantageous tender" (MEAT) or the "lowest cost".
- **Modification of contracts.** Both proposals introduce new rules regulating the modification of contracts during their term and specifying when modifications are acceptable without a new tender procedure.
- **New rules allow procuring entities to include in the contract conditions linked with the contract performance**, such as the reduction of unemployment or the protection of the environment.
- **Improvements to the existing guarantees aimed at combating conflicts of interest, favouritism and corruption.**
- **Creation of a single national oversight body.** The member states will have to designate a single national authority to be in charge of monitoring, implementing and controlling public procurement. It will also be responsible for examining complaints from consumers and business, and transmitting their analysis to the relevant contracting entity.

The adoption of the new proposal should take place before the end of 2012.

The future impact of these proposals in the public procurement internal market – mainly by improving the cost-efficiency of EU public procurement, taking full advantage of all opportunities to deliver the best possible outcomes for the society and creating a real EU public procurement market (rather than the existing 27 national markets) – depends critically on effective implementation.

The above-mentioned new rules proposed by the European Commission have a great potential to eliminate regulatory and natural market barriers (e.g. by harmonising standards/labels, making access to information easier for SMEs and the procedures more proportionate and flexible and helping to eliminate the current regulatory heterogeneity between member states) that presently prevent the public procurement internal market from achieving its full potential. However, the proposed measures will only accomplish these main goals if the member states correctly transpose, implement and enforce the new rules, despite their different administrative capacities.

8. Preventive Approaches

Another class of enforcement methods is 'preventive' in nature. The philosophy here is to develop methods that reduce the likelihood that infringement might occur later. The short verdict on this approach is that it is highly beneficial, and in comparison with infringement procedures, less costly, much faster and probably more effective. These statements would have to be underpinned with hard evidence, of course, even though it is unlikely that one can 'prove' the point empirically. This preventive way of approaching 'barriers' due to bad enforcement, late implementation or wrong interpretation has gradually become far more important over time. As is increasingly the case with the 'pre-infringement' approaches, the *member states* have become central to greater effectiveness in this respect. Hence, both the 'pre-infringement' and the 'preventive' approaches rely more and more, although not only, on the active *cooperation* of member states, as a group, or between the member states and the Commission, in sharp contrast to formal infringement procedures where "the" EU (via the Commission) *opposes* a member state in a legal proceeding.

Ten examples of 'preventive' initiatives or those with a preventive effect (even though the motive for the initiative might be found elsewhere) include:

- Regulatory impact assessments (RIAs)

- Training member states' officials and judges in EU law

- Regular consultation between member state officials negotiating a directive and those (later) responsible for implementation and enforcement

- Disciplining member states in respecting 'mutual recognition'

- Joint (Commission/member states) 'ownership' in implementation (services Directive)

- Inter-member states' cooperation via the IMI system on daily implementation issues

- Council recommendations on member states' implementation and enforcement

- Selective shift in internal market from directives to (EU) regulations

- Directive 98/34 on the prevention of new technical barriers in the internal goods market

- The 'rapid alert' mechanism of Regulation 2679/98, regarding the free movement of goods in case of blockages

This chapter discusses eight of these ten examples, some of them at length (given their importance) and some very briefly.

8.1 Regulatory impact assessment

Regulatory impact assessment (RIA) is the centrepiece of 'Better Regulation' strategies. The European Commission has conducted RIAs since mid-2003, and altogether over 550 had been completed by early 2012. Every piece of draft legislation proposed by the Commission to the EU legislator, such as directives and (EU) regulations, has to be presented together with a RIA, published by the Commission on the same date. The purpose of an RIA is to provide evidence-based and systematic analysis of the European public interest rationale of the proposal, alternative options to accomplish the identified objectives via (a combination of) instruments, an analysis of the economic, environmental and social impacts, including societal benefits and costs, and, where possible, a ranking of the options as well as an explicit treatment of the trade-offs between options. The ultimate aim is to make 'better' EU laws, by avoiding ideological or vested-interest biases and imposing rigorous logic and analysis, to bring in as much empirical evidence as possible (on all options, not just a 'preferred' one), to help MEPs and the Council to think in terms of alternative options (with their expected consequences) and to support public debate in the EU on the basis of solid analysis, data and several alternatives. An RIA does not and should not substitute for decision-making by elected politicians (that is, Council ministers and MEPs). Only the latter are accountable to voters. The idea behind RIAs is not only that the Commission is forced to work within the rigorous and detailed RIA logic, followed by far-reaching transparency, but also that EU-level decision-makers can be held accountable by a much better informed public.

Why do RIAs at EU level form part and parcel of the 'preventive' approaches of better enforcement? There are three reasons. First, RIA procedures[140] impose a duty of consultation with e.g. business and indeed all stakeholders and imply a spirit of openness to comments and suggestions at all stages of the RIA writing (which on average takes some 15 months). Consultations are, more often than not, open and all the internet calls are reported in summary papers by the Commission (all the submissions are on the website as well). It is the combination of open consultation and RIA rigour that tends to result in 'better regulation' – at least, as proposed by the Commission – than before by e.g. blocking exemptions or inconsistencies driven by vested interests or unjustified traditions – and by paying careful attention to solid reasons "why regulate" (the benefits for the EU) and the costs and on whom these fall. This point extends to the instruments and their 'enforceability' in actual practice. Other things being equal, better regulation tends to be more easily enforceable. Of course, this argument may sometimes be undermined by the actual EU laws enacted finally by the Council and the EP together, for whatever political reasons. However, the EP has recently announced that it has established a new unit in its services checking the impact of (non-trivial) amendments to Commission proposals.

Moreover, Malcolm Harbour, Chair of the EP Internal Market and Consumers Affairs Committee, has initiated a policy of first discussing the RIA from the Commission before beginning the debates on the political merits of Commission proposals. Second, the much greater care taken in formulating Commission proposals based on RIAs often has the effect of removing or pre-empting all kinds of technical or legal 'bugs' in legislation that, later, lead to difficulties in implementation and enforcement by member states. Third, every RIA has six stages, the sixth one being monitoring and evaluation of a directive once it is in force. In case implementation or enforcement difficulties can be attributed to a bad, inconsistent or excessively complex directive, the often incorporated review after (say) five years can prompt redrafting, reducing such problems.

---

[140] Over the years since 2002, the Commission's Guidelines for RIAs have improved enormously. For the January 2009 version, see http://ec.europa.eu/governance/impact/docs/key_docs/iag_2009_en.pdf, plus many annexes and several handbooks. For literature, see e.g. Renda (2011) and EU Court of Auditors (2010). For quality assessment of EU RIAs over the last few years, see Fritsch et al. (2012).

8.2   Training member states' officials and judges in EU law

Judges and prosecutors are the main actors in the application of EU law. In that sense, a permanent training of judges and prosecutors is crucial and helps to insure that these actors have a sound understanding of EU law and its mechanisms. According to a recent study commissioned by the European Parliament,[141] there is a high degree of awareness of the relevance of EU law across all member states and an overall impression that the number of cases involving EU law is rising. However, a considerable percentage of the judges interviewed (three-fifths) across the EU said that they don't know how to refer a question to the CJEU at all or that they only know to a minor extent how to do so. Moreover, judges, prosecutors and court staff are more likely to receive continuous training in other subjects than EU law. Just over one-half of the judges and prosecutors who responded to the survey (53%) had received continuous training in EU or another member state's law, but only one-third had done so in the last three years. Only 14% of the judges and prosecutors surveyed said that they had attended a European judicial training programme and 22% had participated in judicial exchanges. No less than 90% of respondents to the survey said they would appreciate measures to promote more contact with judges and/or prosecutors from other member states. The main obstacles faced by judges, prosecutors and court staff to participating in continuous judicial training programmes are: the organisation of the justice system itself (judges may not be replaced during their absence); the lack of information about the training programmes available; short notice of when training programmes will take place; lack of places, particularly for judicial exchanges; lack of funding by employers; institutional opposition; work/life balance and language barriers.

8.3   Regular consultation between those member states' officials negotiating a directive and those (later) responsible for implementation and enforcement

In the early phases of an RIA, there should be consultations between those who draft a directive/regulation (i.e. Commission officials) and those who

---

[141] See "Judicial training in the European Union", European Parliament, Directorate General for Internal Policies, Legal Affairs Committee (http://www.europarl.europa.eu/committees/en/studiesdownload.html?langua geDocument=EN&file=60091).

will later have the responsibility to execute it nationally. Once negotiations start in Council committees, it is even more important for every member state to consult practitioners or officials in the relevant ministries in order to promote a final version of the directive that is relatively easy to implement and enforce, and in any event avoids unnecessary complications that might cause enforcement issues later on, if not 'barriers'. In a classic study of 17 directives as applied in all 12 member states (at the time) (Siedentopf & Ziller, 1988), the lack of contact between negotiators and practitioners proved to be a significant cause for differences in enforcement between member states (hence, 'distortions' in the single market) or occasionally for 'barriers'.

That this is just as much an issue today is clear from the very detailed study made by the Davidson Review (2006, p. 8). Lord Davidson recommends that "there should be an effective transfer of knowledge between teams negotiating and teams implementing European legislation" in order to minimise implementation problems. Admittedly, this is not always easy since, with truly new legislation, there may be few, if any, practitioners available yet. This 'time inconsistency' can be reduced if after the negotiations the negotiating experts are not immediately shifted around to other functions elsewhere inside the public administration. This can avoid the loss of institutional memory and tacit information.

8.4   Disciplining member states in respecting mutual recognition

Mutual recognition in goods markets applies to roughly 21-22% of intra-EU goods trade where EU member states have retained their regulatory autonomy. The remainder is either unregulated (say, the market for teaspoons) or under EU regulation of one kind or another. When EU regulated (to some degree), it is also possible that mutual recognition applies to aspects of such goods that do not fall under EU specifications, hence, where member states retain some discretion. However, when goods are EU regulated (to some degree), one should normally find that the EU legislator has established common objectives. In other words, the thrust of national regulation (under EU directives) is on 'equivalent' (same) objectives and the specifications – when they differ between EU countries – have to be mutually recognised.[142]

---

[142] For details, see Pelkmans (2007 and 2012).

It is extremely hard to 'guesstimate' how much of intra-EU trade in goods enjoys this combination of EU regulation and some national regulatory discretion. In most instances, there will be references to European standards, based on official EU mandates, and this will greatly reduce the possible discrepancies in actual practice as European industry typically produces many goods with explicit consideration of European standards. In some instances, however, the common objectives are not so specific that 'equivalence' between member states is guaranteed. For example, some directives allow member states to add additional requirements that are not subject to mutual recognition – such differentiation beyond EU harmonisation usually indicates that (a few) member states are highly sensitive to particular aspects of (say) food or environmental legislation or details of consumer protection. Such gold plating creates barriers or leaves existing barriers untouched despite harmonisation. This is to be distinguished from gold plating where additional requirements *are* subject to mutual recognition but might still be confusing for cross-border business (when companies do not realise the benefits and rights of mutual recognition).

There are two distinct approaches to mutual recognition. One is the mutual recognition of *existing* provisions in national laws; the other is about pre-empting a lack of national respect for mutual recognition in *new* national legislation at the early drafting stage. Both approaches reduce or prevent what otherwise would be barriers to cross-border business in the internal market. Below we report on the recent, more effective discipline imposed on member states to respect mutual recognition. In section 7.9, the discipline about new draft legislation of member states exercised in the 98/34 Committee is set out in some detail, including extensive empirical evidence.

Mutual recognition of *existing* provisions in national (usually technical) laws that are not based on EU regulation (in EU jargon, the so-called 'non-harmonised' field) has been regulated procedurally in Regulation 764/2008, in force since May 2009. The reason was a simple but important one: European business had lost faith in the proper application of mutual recognition – outside the CJEU court room – by officials from member states who would frequently refer to the specifications of their own domestic laws.[143] This factual neglect of mutual recognition led to high

---

[143] This is documented in Pelkmans (2005) and UNICE (2004), for example.

transaction and compliance costs for cross-border business, the very opposite of what was meant to be stimulated by opportunities inside the single market. Instead, Regulation 764/2008 protects *bona fide* business[144] in the 'non-harmonised' field[145] by imposing procedural obligations on member states and introducing a reversal of the burden of proof now resting on the member state of (intra-EU) importation. Among the several benefits is the much greater assurance to European businesses that they can enter all EU countries with goods falling (partially or entirely) outside EU regulation. This should promote competition in the internal market.

Furthermore, business can (normally) forego the transaction and compliance costs or even the risks of incurring them, which may well stimulate Europeanisation strategies on a wider scale. However, this does not mean a lower level of health or safety (etc.) because member states can of course still intervene if they have a solid case against a particular good – the case ought to be evidence-based (e.g. with testing, etc.) and subject to appeal in courts. Also, the 'rapid alert' mechanisms for (too risky or 'unsafe') food (RASFF) and non-food (RAPEX) goods remain in place, as before. The sole but critical difference, now that Regulation 764/2008 works, is the effective 'protection' of mutual recognition at the moment that it matters most: the prospective or actual access to national markets. This is good news for cross-border business in the EU (or the EEA) and will ultimately translate into benefits of greater choice or variety, possibly lower prices and/or other gains from intra-EU competition.

The actual functioning of this new regime for mutual recognition is monitored closely by the Commission.[146]

---

[144] Bona fide here means a company that can prove its adherence to European standards (including voluntary tests and/or certification) or otherwise technically document the safety (etc.) features of the good and its access to other EU countries.

[145] A non-exhaustive list of goods in the 'non-harmonised field' is available from the Commission at http://ec.europa.eu/enterprise/intsub/a12 .

[146] Note that the Commission facilitates the technical application of Reg. 764/2008 by the provision of 'indicative, non-binding guides' on the application of mutual recognition to precious metals, food supplements, narcotic drugs, firearms, fertilisers and non-CE marked construction products.

8.5   Joint EU and member state ownership of implementation

The 2006/123 horizontal services Directive has been implemented in a unique fashion. In a major effort of profound cooperation between the member states as well as between the member states and the Commission, this complex and ill-drafted Directive[147] has been implemented as much as possible in similar ways, notwithstanding the wide and disruptive encountered variety between EU countries. Such extreme efforts can only be expected in special cases: the services Directive surely is a special case as its scope is broad (applying to services generating close to 40% of EU GNP) and the barriers were numerous and deep-seated, even at several layers of government all the way to provincial and local governments.

The implementation of Directive 2006/123 was guided by four committees (chaired by the Commission, with all member states), a detailed Guide, an obligatory 'screening' of all domestic legislation potentially relevant (literally thousands of laws and decrees at more than one government level), direct monitoring of and support for each and every national implementation by the Commission for years and finally a 'mutual evaluation' (in 2010) amongst the member states. The result is impressive[148] although the actual working of the Directive still has to be proven of course (first report was due in the summer of 2012). There can be no doubt that, following such major and cooperative efforts, numerous enforcement problems in this area have been prevented.

This prominent example shows that proper implementation of complex EU directives is possible in a two-level government system like the EU, only if a) member states are prepared to work together and with the Commission and b) there is a political and administrative conviction of responsible 'ownership' in national capitals. It should be realised that the services Directive is largely based on prior CJEU case law and comprises

---

[147] Legally, the Directive is far from satisfactory in a number of ways, the result of hectic political debates in the EP and the de facto stalemate in the Council. The final text was voted in a marathon session with more than 1,000 amendments without much of a filter of proper legal drafting and of inconsistencies and mistakes. See Barnard (2008) for a detailed exposition of its flaws and weaknesses, and Hatzopoulos (2008) for further analysis.

[148] See COM (2011) 20 of 27 January 2011 on the follow-up of the 'mutual evaluation' and the Commission Staff Working Document SEC (2011) 102 of the same date going into great detail about implementation results.

relatively little 'harmonisation'. Therefore, apart from a number of explicitly banned restrictive practices, which represent great progress for the services market, the Directive's impact hinges mainly on effective domestic screening, the Points of Single Contact (key for business) and effective inter-member states' cooperation in daily matters of administration. In future, some such special cases should utilise similarly intrusive methods in order to accomplish proper implementation and thereby pre-empt many difficulties of later enforcement. That the lessons of the cooperative approach towards the implementation of the services Directive have been learned is clear from two recent initiatives, the IMI system of inter-member state cooperation (see section 8.6) and the new 'partnership' approach between the Commission and the member states with respect to detections of possible misapplication of EU law, signalled via enquiries and complaints.

8.6 Developing the IMI system of inter-member-states' administrative cooperation

In September 2009, the Commission and the member states agreed to establish closer 'partnerships' between the member states (and the Commission as well), with a view to making the single market work better. In many instances this can be important, if not crucial, for business and citizens alike. A breakthrough was accomplished with the start of IMI, the Internal Market Information mechanism, an IT-based information network linking authorities in all 30 EEA countries, with a multilingual search function helping competent authorities find their counterpart in other EU countries, prepared questions and answers in 23 languages as well as automatic translation for other queries. In February 2012, no less than 11,000 authorities were registered in IMI. Its use is rapidly increasing, although currently it is only applied for a) the services Directive and b) the 2005 Directive on recognition of professional qualifications, whereas it may soon be used for public procurement questions (and possibly, posted workers).

For a long time in the EU, inter-member state administrative cooperation was a serious weakness: slow, ineffective or even failing hopelessly, leading to business frustration and loss of opportunities. IMI is very different. In numerous trivial instances, like the verification of addresses or registrations or licenses or diplomas, it works rapidly (often requiring only days, 43% processed in a week). It seems promising. The Commission proposal for a firm legal basis[149] had received strong support from the European Parliament. IMI has the additional advantage that it has now become routine for national or regional administrations to work together with counterparts in other member states. Although it is exceedingly difficult to foresee all the benefits flowing from a successful and widespread utilisation of IMI in more fields, it is bound to be advantageous for cross-border business and has the potential to pre-empt high information and transaction costs. In case of administrative issues, the key business problem of the past – losing time-to-market – may be drastically reduced as well.

8.7 Selective shift from internal market directives to EU regulations

According to the Internal Market Scoreboard (No. 23, September 2011), on 30 April 2011, the internal market *acquis* consisted of 1,525 directives and 1,347 EU regulations.[150] These seemingly plain data mask a silent revolution in the EU internal market regulatory regime. Over the last decade or so, the total number of internal market directives has hardly changed whereas the number of EU regulations has increased enormously, indeed, has more than quadrupled! Thus, in Scoreboard No. 10 (May 2002), the total number of directives was the same as ten years later (1,497, as against 1,525 in the spring of 2011) but the total number of EU regulations amounted to no more than 299 (as against 1,347 in 2011).

For the subject of this study, namely enforcement in the internal market, this major shift can be regarded as another instance of a 'preventive' approach. After all, regulations have direct effect and need no transposition into member states' domestic law; there is, by definition, no implementation problem. Although the authors have no hard proof, it is likely that EU regulations also lead to fewer problems of wrong or misguided problems of application of EU law. In other words, enforcement in the internal market is expected to improve significantly, if and to the extent that regulations rather than directives are employed. And, as noted, since 2002, the extent of the shift has been very large indeed. This means

---

[149] COM (2010) 522 of 29 August 2011 on the IMI Regulation.

[150] Not counting decisions, recommendations and other softer EU law, and CJEU rulings.

that, irrespective of the transposition deficit and also irrespective of the compliance deficit (see section 5.3), enforcement in the internal market must have improved solely on account of having far more EU regulations. Curiously, this shift has remained largely unnoticed and is never explicitly related to 'better enforcement' efforts.

The authors have not analysed the roots of this shift. But a few suggestions can be made. First, there have been instances of substitution between directives and EU regulations, once directives came up for review or revision. Examples include the two new proposed regulations on the approval and market surveillance of two- or three-wheel vehicles and quadric-cycles[151] and of tractors and forestry vehicles,[152] respectively, and the change from Directive 95/46 on personal data protection to Regulation 1882/2003. Second, new legislative initiatives have, more often than before, been proposed and enacted in the form of regulations. A prominent example is the mutual recognition Regulation 764/2008. There may be other reasons as well.

At the same time, one wonders why the number of directives has not increased over ten years. This is mainly due to a series of consolidation initiatives (for example, Directive 2005/36 on professional qualifications brings together 15 earlier directives on separate professions) besides 'better regulation' initiatives, which have led to the removal of entire families of directives (such as 30 directives on sizes and shapes of vegetables and fruits, and a few so-called 'recipe' directives on tea, honey, coffee, etc.). The REACH Regulation 1907/2006 forms a combination of the two, substituting for one Council directive and four Commission directives.

The shift to regulations, with the clear and explicit approval of member states, can be considered as a highly significant contribution to better enforcement in the internal market.

8.8   EU prevention of new technical barriers (Directive 98/34/EC)

8.8.1   A credible discipline of national technical regulation

Under Directive 98/34/EC (revised twice since, and formerly known as 83/189), the European Commission receives compulsory notifications from the member states of all national draft laws containing technical regulations

---

[151] COM(2010) 542 final.

[152] COM(2010) 0395 final.

(on goods and, a minor part on information services). The notified national draft laws are verified so as to enable the Commission as well as the member states to detect potential (new) technical barriers or other (new) regulatory barriers to intra-EU cross-border trade. Subsequently, the Commission requests the relevant member states to amend the draft in such a way as to *prevent* such (potential) barriers.

This unique and most remarkable instrument has protected the internal goods market from becoming a mockery over time. The Directive 98/34/EC mechanism is remarkable for at least two reasons. First, member states temporarily renounce their sovereign right and freedom to legislate as and when they want. A notification automatically postpones the conclusion of domestic pre-legislative procedures for three months, i.e. the draft cannot be adopted before the end of this standstill period. Depending on the situation, however, such standstill period may be prolonged and take four to six months. In case of a blockage (i.e. when the Commission announces that the proposal concerns a matter that is covered by a proposal for a directive, regulation or decision), it may reach 12 months. If the Council adopts a common position, the national legislative procedure is blocked for 18 months. This is a credible way to prevent new technical barriers from arising. Second, notification is not only compulsory but the CJEU has explicitly ruled (in *CIA Security v Signalson and Securitel*, 1996) that non-notification renders the national law adopted subsequently 'unenforceable'. Again, this ruling provides strong incentives to notify, thereby raising credibility of the Directive even further.

What is typically notified? Basically, all technical regulations together with an explanation of the necessity to make such regulations, if this is not clear in the draft, unless the regulations are a simple transposition of international or European standards. It is hard to 'guesstimate' what the economic significance of this domain is, but a rough proxy would be at least around 20% of intra-EU trade in goods. However, one has to appreciate the precise meaning of this. The regular Commission reports on Directive 98/34/EC[153] speak of goods in the non-harmonised field as well as in the harmonised field. The latter refer to secondary national legislation which elaborates principles and specifications in EU directives – depending on the situation, the member states have considerable discretion here, and

---

[153] Such as the latest ones: COM(2009) 690 of 21 December 2009 (on 2006 – 2008) and COM (2011) 853 of 7 December 2011 (on 2009 and 2010), for example.

in the 98/34 procedure it is verified whether that discretion is not used in ways that create unnecessary divergences or incompatibilities with the directive(s). In other words, it disciplines at EU level the national regulatory autonomy first received in the Directive, such that no new barriers to internal market emerge.

8.8.2   The amazing record of 98/34: Empirical trends

Just how critical the 98/34 mechanism is for the protection of the internal goods market can be read from Figures 22 and 23 showing the notifications over the period 1988-2010. The regulatory activity of member states is considerable. In the period of the EU-12 (1988-1994), annual notifications hovered between 300 and 400 and many of these prompted observations from the Commission and/or member states, suspecting potential barriers. During the period of the EU-15 (1995-2003), notifications start rising to (sometimes far) beyond 500 a year.[154] A further structural increase can be observed after the first and second Eastern enlargement (2004-2010), approaching an annual average of around 700 a year.

Figure 22. Total number of notifications of national draft laws under 98/34, 1988-98

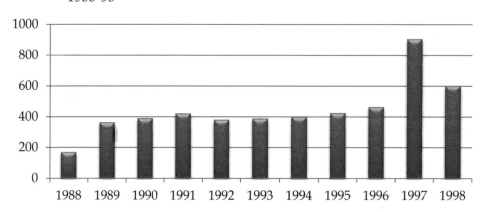

Source: Pelkmans et al. (2000, p. 274), based on Commission reports.

---

[154] The extreme peak in 1997 is due to the Netherlands, suddenly realising the consequences of the CIA Security case. It was catching up in 1997 with 400 extra notifications that it first felt were unnecessary. For details of this 'regulatory-crisis', see Box 1 in Pelkmans et al. (2000, pp. 270-271).

Figure 23. Total number of notifications of national draft laws under 98/34, 1999-2010

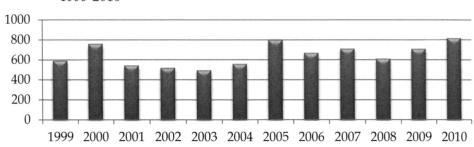

Notes: 2004: Enlargement from EU-15 to EU-25; 2007: Enlargement from EU-25 to EU-27.

Sources: Pelkmans (2007); SEC (2009) 1704 of 21 December 2009 and SEC(2011) 1509 of 7 December 2011.

In short, for already one and a half decades, the number of annual notifications exceeded 500, with a recent trend of 700 a year. This amounts to unique empirical evidence of the high, if not secularly increasing, regulatory activity of member states. In Europe the shift to more and more EU regulation, at the expense of national regulation (at least in goods), is frequently discussed. This trend is widely accepted as inevitable given the ambition of creating and maintaining a deep and smoothly functioning internal (here: goods and services) market. One of the repercussions is that member states (as well as businesses and even citizens) have (rightly) become quite sensitive to the need for EU regulation to be carefully justified, least-cost and well-designed based on strict RIAs.

What is rarely considered, however, is what member states themselves do in the areas remaining under national regulatory autonomy, for the simple reason that there is no easy way to 'observe' such trends. The 98/34 mechanism gives analysts unique (although partial, for goods only) empirical evidence about how member states use their autonomy in goods markets. The inference is clear: member states remain eager regulators. Yet, this eagerness creates serious risks of newly emerging technical or other regulatory barriers, which might be difficult, slow and costly to remove again. Hence, the justification of the intrusive 98/34 mechanism which does not reduce national regulatory autonomy but disciplines it for the sake of the internal goods market. It is important that the member states jointly have assumed 'ownership' since they all can (and do) make observations on the draft laws of other member states, whilst being disciplined themselves as well.

The effectiveness of 98/34 in protecting the internal goods market can be appreciated once one 'zooms in' on the actual working of the Commission. No less than some 12,500 notifications have been dealt with since 1988. One might assume that once the mechanism is well-known inside the national administration (between ministries – which requires coordination done in practice by national enquiry points), the mere existence of the mechanism should already exercise some disciplinary effect. Thus, one should expect the potential barriers detected in 98/34 procedures to be a good deal fewer (in terms of draft laws)[155] than 12,500. Even so, thousands of potential barriers have been prevented in these 23 years for which Figures 22 and 23 show data. The 98/34 procedure allows greater precision with respect to the number of prevented barriers. Member states and the Commission can make two types of observations on notified draft laws: *comments*, mainly requests for clarification so as to avoid interpretations or execution leading to possible barriers; and *detailed opinions*, in case a potential barrier is identified, leading to therefore an automatic suspension of the adoption of the draft for another three months.[156]

Figure 24 provides the evidence for the period 2004-10 inclusively. The number of comments over these seven years amount to 1,142 for the member states and 1,113 for the Commission. Even if one (rather generously) assumes that none of these instances would have given rise to later barriers, the procedure undoubtedly increases legal certainty for business, which is a much appreciated gain (lowering information costs). Were one to assume that some of the draft laws having been 'commented' on would have given rise to barriers, the beneficial impact of 98/34 would be so much bigger. It seems reasonable to presume that the latter assumption is probably correct.

---

[155] Of course, a single draft law may well contain more than one or indeed many (potential) technical barriers. Here, we simplify by assuming that one law can be tantamount to one (potential) barrier.

[156] The Commission can also block a draft law in case relevant harmonisation work is already under way or due to be undertaken. This leads to a suspension for 12 months, giving time for the preparation of a draft directive.

Figure 24. Detection under 98/34 of potential regulatory barriers, 2004-10

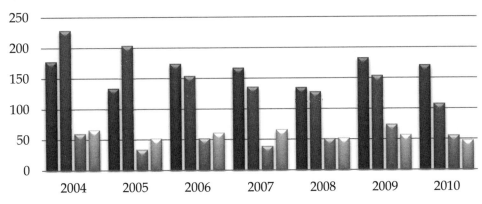

■ MS comments ■ COM comments ■ MS det. Opinion ■ COM det. Opinion

Sources: SEC(2007)350 of 21 March 2007, SEC(2009)1704 of 21 December 2009 and
SEC(2011)1509 of 7 December 2011.

The 'detailed opinions' identify potential future barriers. The member states identified over the seven years no less than 366 such instances, and the Commission 402. One cannot add these totals because many detailed opinions of member states may well be on the same draft laws and are likely to overlap with detailed opinions from the Commission; usually, the Commission's list is larger than the number of draft laws identified as problematic by member states. On this basis, one can conclude that no less than 400 national draft laws were temporarily stopped by detailed opinions, indicating a serious risk of emerging technical barriers in the internal goods market. Moreover, the experience shows that a significant chunk of identified potential problems can be solved in a dialogue between the notifying member state and the Commission or another member state that issued a comment or a detailed opinion.

This amazing record shows how crucial 98/34 is for keeping the internal market from deteriorating by preventing a groundswell of new technical barriers. With even more detailed data below, we shall construct and calculate an *effective prevention indicator* showing the proven performance of 98/34 in pre-empting what otherwise would have become 'new' barriers in the single goods market. This prevention comes in addition to the probably growing awareness and increased discipline inside ministries and the deterrence effect of notification and analysis by other member states and the Commission.

8.8.3 The most recent empirical evidence on 98/34

We provide empirical evidence for 2011 separately. This is subject to caveats. The data shown in this subsection are taken from the TRIS database[157] as it stood in mid-March 2012. However, because some notifications are under periods of commenting or 'detailed opinions' longer than three months, the data cannot be final until much later into the year 2012. Therefore, the data can serve as a reasonably good proxy of the trend in 2011, but their exact numbers might appear to differ somewhat, later on.

The number of notifications declined in 2011 to 675, from 817 in 2010. The 2011 figure is roughly at the average level since 2005, showing a stable trend line. Figure 25 demonstrates that EU member states exhibit considerable differences in their propensity to notify in years 2010-11, that is, to regulate either in the non-harmonised or harmonised field or in both. Whereas 10 EU countries notified 20 draft laws or less over the two years together, four member states reach beyond 100, with a peak of 162 notifications by France.

Figure 25. Total number of notifications - breakdown by country, 2010-11

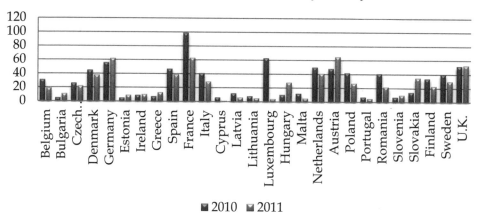

■ 2010   ■ 2011

Table 11 highlights these disparities between member states' notifications in percentages. No less than 11 member states recorded more

---

[157] TRIS, which stands for Technical Regulations Information System, is a database that facilitates the notification system under Directive 98/34/EC. On the publicly available website, the public can find all the relevant information on the procedure, including notified draft laws and can subscribe to a regular alert system on the latest notifications.

than 5% of the total 2010 notifications; in 2011 this group shrank to seven EU countries, signalling a more evenly spread pattern of notifications.

Table 11. Percentages of notifications submitted by member state, 2010-11

Country	2010	2011
Belgium	3.79%	2.81%
Bulgaria	0.61%	1.63%
Czech Republic	3.18%	3.26%
Denmark	5.51%	5.63%
Germany	6.85%	9.19%
Estonia	0.61%	1.33%
Ireland	1.1%	1.48%
Greece	0.86%	1.93%
Spain	5.75%	5.78%
France	12.12%	9.33%
Italy	5.02%	4.3%
Cyprus	0.73%	0.15%
Latvia	1.47%	0.89%
Lithuania	0.98%	0.74%
Luxembourg	7.71%	0.59%
Hungary	1.22%	4.15%
Malta	1.47%	0.74%
Netherlands	6.12%	6.07%
Austria	5.88%	9.63%
Poland	5.14%	4.0%
Portugal	0.86%	0.74%
Romania	5.75%	3.26%
Slovenia	0.86%	1.48%
Slovakia	1.71%	5.19%
Finland	4.16%	3.4%
Sweden	4.90%	4.44%
United Kingdom	6.36%	7.85%

In the reactions on notifications, there is a possibly interesting discrepancy between the Commission and the member states. Whereas the Commission seems to have become more vigilant and/or the projects notified were more problematic (comments going up from 108 in 2010 to 112 in 2011, despite fewer notifications, and detailed opinions going up from 48[158] to 56), the member states' responses decreased in number, in line with the decline of the total (comments decreasing from 176 in 2010 to 147 in 2011, and detailed opinions going down as well from 49 in 2010 to 46 in 2011).

8.8.4 Proven prevention, empirical evidence for 2010 and 2011

The effectiveness of 98/34 is exerted in three ways. One is through the very existence of the mechanism for more than 25 years now, which is bound to have induced some degree of discipline and efforts to ensure EU legal compatibility in ministries in all EU member states. The second way is via the working of the 98/34 notification procedure, which has gradually engendered a greater 'Europeanisation' of domestic law-making by the permanent machinery to comment on drafts of other EU countries, and to identify instances of potential and likely 'barriers' springing from draft laws which have no mutual recognition clauses or comprise other (too) restrictive ways to pursue health, safety or environmental objectives. These two beneficial effects of 98/34 cannot be empirically verified in any meaningful fashion, although this does not mean that such impacts are not real.

A third effect can be verified empirically with the help of three proxy measures. We refer to *barriers that were actually prevented* via the comments and especially the detailed opinions. In the following we assume, for the sake of simplicity, that a detailed opinion is tantamount to 'a barrier prevented' which is in actual practice very often the case. More generally, comments may also point to issues or a potential for later problems or overly complicated or heavy bureaucracy, etc., but comments may just as well provide advice or comparisons with solutions found elsewhere. By zooming in on comments and in particular, on detailed opinions, it is

---

[158] Note that there were 48 draft regulations notified to the European Commission in 2010 that were issued with a detailed opinion from the European Commission. However, of these 48 detailed opinions, only 44 were issued by the Commission in 2010. Only those 44 detailed opinions issued by the Commission in 2010 are analysed in section 8.8.6.

possible to calculate the *'proven prevention'* in the annual functioning of the 98/34 procedure. The empirical perspective can be provided with the help of three indicators. The first one is the gross detection rate (GDR), showing the reported activities (though not in substantive detail) of the procedure in detecting issues, problems and/or likely barriers. The GDR is the ratio of the sum of the comments and detailed opinions of one year, divided by the total number of notifications.

The gross prevention indicator (GPI) focuses on prevention we are pretty sure about, that is, the share in percentages of all detailed opinions in all notifications in one year. However, the GPI is "gross" because, although it is relatively easy to calculate from the TRIS website, it cannot be fully precise in identifying how many new barriers have been prevented per year (assuming that one draft law is tantamount to one barrier). The reason is that more than one member state can have a detailed opinion on the same notified draft law and/or that a member state as well as the Commission may file a detailed opinion on the same draft law. The effective prevention indicator (EPI) filters out such double counting from the calculation. The GPI is the share (in %) of the notifications that have attracted one or more detailed opinions. In Figure 26 this empirical perspective has been brought together for the last few years: the GDR for 2004-11, the GPI for 2004-11 and the EPI for 2010 and 2011.

Figure 26. Detection and effective prevention of barriers in 98/34

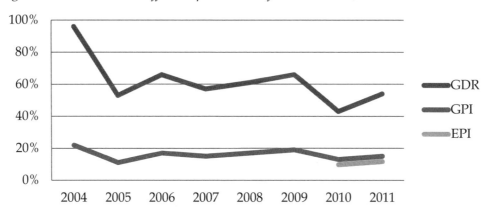

Legend: GDR = Gross Detection Rate; GPI = Gross Prevention Indicator; and EPI = Effective Prevention Indicator.

Figure 26 shows immediately that, after many years of having the Directive 98/34/EC and supporting CJEU case law, such as Unilever and

CIA Security, the trend is that still around one-half of the notified draft laws lead to an issuance of either comments or detailed opinions or both (2004 was the first enlargement year and is an outlier). When it comes to identified (likely) barriers in national draft laws, the scores are much lower. Nonetheless, the GPI hovers around 15% or so, which is far from trivial. After filtering this, the EPI for 2010 and 2011 shows respectively 9.7% and 11.7% (in absolute numbers, in both years). These are good proxies of actually prevented barriers to intra-EU goods trade. Figure 26 offers firm evidence of the value of a credible and intrusive mechanism such as procedure 98/34 to pre-empt the steady erosion of the internal market for goods.

8.8.5   Sectoral technical barriers, prevented (2010, 2011)[159]

Agriculture and foodstuff was the sector that saw the highest number of notifications issued with comments and/or detailed opinions (134 notified draft regulations) over the period 2010-11 (see Annex I and II). The subjects covered included, among others, labelling of foodstuffs, food supplements, origin of products, food hygiene, composition of foodstuffs and beverages, materials intended to come into contact with foodstuffs, mineral, spring and drinking waters for human consumption, equipment for treatment of water for human consumption and measures on genetically modified organisms (GMOs). EU legislation on GMOs includes, inter alia, the Directive 2001/18/EC[160] on the deliberate release into the environment of genetically modified organisms, Regulation (EC) No 1829/2003[161] on genetically modified food and feed, Regulation (EC) No 1830/2003[162] on the traceability of food and feed products produced from genetically modified

---

[159] In this section, we only consider the TRIS notifications issued with a detailed opinion and/or a comment, by the Commission or the member states.

[160] Directive 2001/18/EC of the European Parliament and of the Council of 12 March 2001 on the deliberate release into the environment of genetically modified organisms and repealing Council Directive 90/220/EC.

[161] Regulation (EC) No 1829/2003 of the European Parliament and of the Council of 22 September 2003 on genetically food and feed.

[162] Regulation (EC) No 1830/2003 of the European Parliament and of the Council of 22 September 2003, concerning the traceability and labelling of genetically modified organisms and the traceability of food and feed products produced from genetically modified organisms and amending Directive 2001/18/EC.

organisms and the Commission's Recommendation on co-existence measures 2010/C 200/01.[163]

A high number of draft technical regulations in the field of **building and construction**, during the reported period, were also issued with detailed opinions/comments by the Commission and the member states (68 notified draft regulations). A great part of these draft notified regulations are related to firefighting equipment, supporting structures made from concrete, dangerous substances, their properties and labelling. The building and construction sector is regulated at EU level by Directive 89/106/EEC[164] on construction products and Directive 2010/31/EU.[165] Classification, packaging and labelling of dangerous preparations are regulated in Regulation (EC) No 1272/2008.[166]

The third sector with a higher number of notified draft regulations issued with detail opinions and/or comments was **telecommunications** (47 notified draft regulations), mainly concerned with radio interfaces. This is a sector in which rapid technology developments in recent years have resulted in increasingly complex national regulations, which could potentially create barriers within the internal market.

During this period (2010-11), we also observed a great number of notified draft regulations issued with comments and/or detailed opinions related to transport (45), mechanics (39), environment and packaging (30).

---

[163] Commission Recommendation 2010/C 200/01, of 13 July 2010, on guidelines for the development of national co-existence measures to avoid the unintended presence of GMOs in conventional and organic crops.

[164] Directive 89/106/EEC Council Directive of 21 December 1988 on the approximation of laws, regulations and administrative provisions of the member states relating to construction products.

[165] Directive 2010/31/EU of the European Parliament and of the Council of 19 May 2010, on the energy performance of buildings.

[166] Regulation (EC) No 1272/2008 of the European Parliament and of the Council of 16 December 2008, on classification, labelling and packaging of substances and mixtures (REACH), amending and repealing Directives 67/548/EEC and 1999/45/EC, and amending Regulation (EC) No 1907/2006.

8.8.6 *Further analysis of 2010 TRIS notifications 98/34 issued with a detailed opinion by the Commission*

Annex III provides a somewhat greater detail of 43 of the 44 detailed opinions issued by the Commission in 2010. This number of detailed opinions amounts to less than 6% of the 817 notifications that year. The main purpose of Annex III is to find out what kind of potential 'barriers' to the internal market or infringements the Commission is objecting to within the preventive framework of Directive 98/34/EC and to acquire a sense of how significant such potential barriers are in the internal market for goods. Of course, the table refers only to one single year, which entails some limitations for the purposes of this analysis. On the basis of these limited data, we draw the conclusions presented below from Annex III.

a) Detailed opinions are a powerful indicator that barriers might arise, if the notified national draft laws subject to such an opinion would not be changed. The utility for the single market of the 98/34 procedure and follow-up becomes even more clear once one is able to study the notifications and detailed opinions in greater detail. The potential infringements are found in highly specialised submarkets (which might easily go unnoticed without such a notification obligation) as well as in more sizeable markets (e.g. gambling, building products, foodstuffs, batteries & accumulators, fuels) where the economic impact is of course likely to be more important. The analysis indicates also that quite often, the absence of a 'mutual recognition' clause is the principal issue that would create a barrier to internal market.

b) Knowing the history of Directive 98/34/EC (see e.g. the survey by Pelkmans et al., 2000), it is striking to find that, much like 10 or 20 years ago, it seems difficult for national ministries, and for units inside national ministries, to master and understand EU law, or at least the basics with respect to the free movement of goods and the 'New Approach'. Many of the same types of mistakes or 'failures to think internal market' still show up today. However, it must be noted that cooperation of national ministries with national enquiry points set up to coordinate nationally the procedure under Directive 98/34/EC has improved the awareness of the notification procedure. Moreover, it may be observed that indeed some learning *has* taken place in the meantime: from 1995-98 (when the EU had only 15 member states as compared to 27 in 2010), the number of the Commission's detailed opinions amounted to (respectively) 75, 105, 118 and 62, all far above the 44 in 2010 for more countries.

c) The notion of 'mutual recognition' in non-harmonised areas still appears to be 'underused' by national ministries and regulators, demonstrating the utility and preventive effect of Directive 98/34/EC.

d) Occasionally, national administrations may not appreciate the crucial difference between a 'presumption of compliance' that an EN standard (recognised and published by the Commission) confers on a product under the New Approach, from making a (EN or European) standard compulsory under national law (thereby, going against the spirit of the New Approach and blocking the internal market as well as innovation).

e) Cases in agriculture and food and related (phyto)sanitary issues often tend to be regulated in an approach quite distinct from the New Approach or mutual recognition; detailed directives nevertheless leave some discretion to member states (hence, less than full harmonisation) and the inclination to use that discretion is found to be fairly strong. This might lead member states to interpret the national discretion more widely than it legally is, under such directives, which may, in turn lead to cases about the scope of a directive or about details in national (draft) laws which might conflict with the harmonised elements.

f) From an historical point of view, many of the detailed opinions used to concern the so-called 'non-harmonised' sectors and therefore very often requested the insertion of a mutual recognition clause. Although the cases of missing mutual recognition clauses are still present, one can observe a gradual shift towards problems with directives of total or partial harmonisation. This shift signifies that Directive 98/34/EC has additionally become, much more than in the past, a special monitor of the implementation of EU directives in the range of technical national laws and decrees (in addition to mutual recognition issues).

g) As to the sectoral composition of the Commission's detailed opinions issued in 2010, one might raise a question whether the three most important sectors in the notifications issued with comments and/or detailed opinions for 2010 and 2011 (agro-food, mechanics and building and construction)[167] also stand out in the Commission's written objections. This is the case for the agro-food sector, which leads in the Commission's detailed opinions as well (12 objections), and 'mechanics' (4), but not the case for the building and construction sector. Indeed, the second sector issued with more Commission detailed opinions in 2010 is transport (7).

---

[167] See section 7.8.5.

9. REDUCING TRANSACTION AND INFORMATION COSTS

A third challenge in enforcing the EU market arises from the need to reduce the transaction and information costs of actual or potential market access, including legal uncertainty. Whether intentional or not, these costs can be regarded as barriers or border effects for business and there is every reason to lower them in a single market. Among the Commission's initiatives/mechanisms that could contribute to reducing transactions and information costs, we can mention the following:

- Commission guidelines, interpretative notes, handbooks, etc.;
- Points of single contact (e.g. services Directive and the new legislative framework);
- Commission information flow (websites, EU Info Centres, etc.);
- Cheaper/easier cross-border dispute settlements (FIN-NET, ADR) and
- 28th regime for contract law.

Not only has the Commission (helped by the internet) become far more active and forthcoming in disseminating detailed information, an increasing number of EU laws are explained in plain terms via a range of Commission websites (indeed, a consolidation of these might be desirable for business) and phone numbers. EU Info Centres have also arisen in all member states and e.g. the services Directive requires (free) Points of Single Contact, on which business is very keen. The direct effect of these services is meant to lower transaction and information costs, but the indirect effect of Single Contact Points on member states' administrations is likely to be a far better and directly available EU knowledge, which, in turn, raises the quality of local enforcement and reduces the probability of incorrect interpretations.

A new twist to this cost reduction approach (which also has a 'preventive' element to it) are recent attempts to develop EU instruments that lower the costs and risks of EU-wide transactions. One set of attempts is about cheaper/easier cross-border dispute settlements, e.g. FIN-NET, the network for financial services, and the recent Commission proposals on Alternative Dispute Resolution (ADR) and online dispute resolution (ODR).[168] Alternative dispute settlement mechanisms may also complement the traditional judicial system by facilitating the resolution of conflicts and avoiding costly procedures.

According to a recent study,[169] there are 750 ADR schemes handling consumer disputes across the EU. However, geographical and sectoral gaps in the coverage were still identified. It clearly leads to disparities in the accessibility of effective ADR. Moreover, ADR schemes as a rule do not accept complaints against traders in *other* member states. Recent studies also show that the number of disputes submitted to ADR is increasing, but is still small. Indeed, only 5% of the EU consumers took their case to an ADR entity in 2010, and only 9% of businesses report ever having used ADR. In order to promote the use of the ADR and create effective, impartial and transparent ADR schemes, the European Commission made a new proposal in November 2011 on alternative and online dispute resolution (ADR and ODR platform).[170] The proposed Directive on consumer ADR will cover all kinds of consumer disputes and aims to provide consumers and businesses, particular small ones, with a out-of-court, low-cost (ADR procedures must be free of charge for consumers or have a cost below €50),

---

[168] Proposal for a Directive of the European Parliament and of the Council on alternative dispute resolution for consumer disputes and amending Regulation No 2006/2004 and Directive 2009/22/EC (Directive on consumer ADR), COM (2011) 793/2 and proposal for a Regulation of the European Parliament and of the Council on online dispute resolution for consumer disputes (Regulation on consumer ODR), (SEC (2011) 14, both from 29.11.2011.

[169] "Use of Alternative Dispute Resolution in the European Union", Final Report to the European Commission – DG Sanco, 16 October 2009. See also, "Cross-border Alternative Dispute Resolution in the European Union", European Parliament Internal Market and Consumer Affairs Committee, 2011 (http://www.europarl.europa.eu/meetdocs/2009_2014/documents/imco/dv/ad r_study_/adr_study_en.pdf).

[170] The proposals form part of the 12 key actions of the Single Market Act and the "Europe 2020 Strategy".

fast (most disputes submitted to ARD are decided within 90 days) and alternative way to improve redress in the internal market. The draft proposal covers contractual disputes between consumers and traders of services or goods. This only covers business-to-consumer (B2C) disputes. Business-to-business (B2B) disputes are excluded from the scope of the proposed legislation. Furthermore, to avoid imposing excessive costs and burdens on the member states, the Commission proposal will be built on the entities already existing in the member states. The proposed regulation on consumer ODR aims to cover the existing gap of ADR for shopping online and will create an EU-wide online platform, providing consumers and businesses with a single point of entry to resolve their disputes concerning purchases made online. This single European point of entry will automatically send the consumer's complaint to the national ADR entity.

It's also important to develop European networks of ADR entities, in order to facilitate the cross-border resolution of disputes, e.g. FIN-NET, the network for financial services.

Another set of attempts seeks to enact at EU level a 28th regime for contract law, meant to promote legal certainty for business in the single market. A proposal has been made for sales law[171] and one is expected for insurance. If the 28th regime is attractive enough, it reduces 'regulatory heterogeneity' among member states. In fact, contracts are essential for running a business and the existence of a 28th contract law for cross-border transactions might not only promote cross-border trade, but also legal certainty and the uniform implementation of EU law. The proposed regulation would create a 28th optional European contract law for the sale of goods, with contracts for the sale of goods applying both to B2B and B2C transactions (previous agreement of both parts is necessary).

---

[171] Proposal for a Regulation of the European Parliament and of the Council on a Common European Sales Law, COM (2011) 635 final.

10. RECOMMENDATIONS

T here can be no doubt about the firmer resolve, evident for around a decade or so, and about the widening and strengthening of efforts with respect to implementation and proper application of EU internal market law by both the European Commission and the member states. While of course retaining the ultimate legal option of going to the Court of Justice of the European Union (CJEU) for infringement cases, it is – rightly – considered to be (much) faster and mostly cheaper to employ a range of other approaches in order to avoid the route all the way to the Luxembourg court, or, to prevent bad implementation and/or application in the first place. The keywords for these newer methods are 'informal' approaches and 'cooperative' relations between the member states and the Commission, and not litigation emphasising conflicting views. To the extent that EU member states assume 'ownership' of resolving implementation and application issues, the 'cooperative' methods of working in various ways to prevent or avoid heavy and slow infringement procedures or to lower information and transaction costs of effective market access for businesses tend to be superior in most instances.

All this is not just about EU law enforcement but also about the confidence European business develops and maintains in the genuine opportunities offered by the single market, unhindered by improper implementation or application of EU laws, or unnecessarily bureaucratic and disproportionate problems of intra-EU market access in numerous ways. It is equally crucial for European consumers eager to make use of the many opportunities offered in terms of choice, speed and prices of cross-border exchange of goods or services. As the CJEU has noted many times, in the final analysis, the internal EU market is to be considered as a 'domestic market'. In other words, except for clearly justified derogations allowing discretion and regulatory autonomy of member states, there should be no hindrances in 'doing business cross-border' (B2B) or indeed conducting B2C and C2C exchanges throughout the EU-27 or the EEA.

However, now that the resolve is greater and several new methods have been introduced with some measure of success, the last thing one should do is to consider the enforcement in the internal market as a problem solved. It is not. As the European Business Test Panel (2009) shows, European business is still not convinced that cross-border exchanges are easy and well-received by other governments. That mere fact alone already throttles entrepreneurial initiatives and the active search for opportunities in other national markets. Moreover, as our study has shown in detail, there are still lots of enforcement problems, big and small, and almost every new method would seem to attract new notifications or complaints. Much of that is resolved, which is certainly good news and can be expected to stimulate, sooner or later, further business action, whether trade or investment. In turn, this is likely to heighten competitive rivalry throughout the internal market, which is a source of economic growth. Altogether, this blend of good and bad news about enforcement can only serve as an encouragement to pursue a path which, apparently, begins to pay off in terms of better enforcement. This should increase consumer welfare directly or indirectly and usually improve competitive conditions, stimulating growth.

In light of these very real and potential benefits, we suggest the following **_recommendations_** for the European Commission and the member states:

1. The widening of enforcement from formal infringement procedures to a broader spectrum, including different pre-infringement routes, a range of preventive initiatives and efforts to reduce transaction and information costs about national regulation as well, are strongly encouraged. This is best done by pursuing a more general _EU enforcement strategy_ encompassing all these elements, with many Commission DGs and the member states involved, each with well-defined roles but in a cooperative spirit. Such a strategy should be carefully considered and our study cannot be the only basis for its formulation. Nevertheless, we suggest that legal aspects should not dominate the strategy. A successful enforcement strategy hinges at least as much on the right incentives (or the absence of disincentives) for complainants, speed (in most cases), resources (e.g. for SOLVIT), costs and benefits of detection and of different resolution mechanisms. Perfect enforcement is, unfortunately, an illusion. Imperfect enforcement implies that, to some extent, choices can be made, for instance, making relatively more effort to accomplish a (much) better functioning internal market, as this may help to fuel economic growth.

2. The idea that the European Commission is the 'guardian of the treaty' against a flood of cases from unwilling member states has, for much too long, been regarded as the foundation of effective enforcement of EU (internal market) law. It risks creating a habit of litigation, also in the many instances where the cooperative route would express the collective character of the European public good, be it the internal market or other *acquis* of the Union. EU countries have every interest in a well-functioning internal market and so have their companies and consumers. The notion of 'partnership' between the Commission and the member states naturally fits the roles of both in the EU system and can stimulate effective problem-solving in a variety of ways. Member states should embrace more firmly their 'ownership' of the EU *acquis*, and in particular, the single market: the positive experiences in SOLVIT, EU Pilot and the 98/34 Committee have already helped a lot to improve enforcement. It is far more fruitful to consider the 'guardian' function first as a duty to monitor, inspect and detect, and, second, to set in motion whatever resolution mechanism can be effective. It is only when cooperative or 'informal' resolution mechanisms fail that the 'guardian' function ought to be interpreted as litigation. Being the 'guardian' is thus nothing else than accomplishing the *best possible enforcement*, because that is in the interest of the Union and its economy. Infringement procedures cannot bring the best possible enforcement, given disincentives like the huge delays as well as the costs per case. Moreover, it is a fact, also underlined by the empirical evidence in this study, that infringement procedures can never deal with more than a small fraction of suspected infringements. Litigation is an ultimate remedy, indispensable for credibility, but far from central when trying to improve the functioning of the internal market via better enforcement.

3. SOLVIT is a success story since it has proven to be a resolution mechanism with easy access, a high success rate and considerable speed, while costing very little. The resources provided by member states are unequal, but too many member states still ought to bring their SOLVIT budget up to required minima. The investment involved is very small, usually a few full-time equivalent (FTE) personnel. Given present austerity, it is likely to be inevitable that member states can only be seen to do this if minimum staffing is regulated at EU level.

4. A closer study of business cases in SOLVIT and of business attitudes towards this free mechanism with limited and voluntary solutions suggests that SOLVIT should focus on SMEs in the first place. The idea of making SOLVIT more attractive to business may work for cases like VAT disbursement, but would require more e.g. for free movement of goods and

of services. Promoting SOLVIT in business circles is useful, yet one has to consider this also in the light of what alternatives for rapid enforcement business disposes of, in contrast to most problems for citizens.

5. The Commission's Scoreboards have proven their utility over the last 15 years or so. The average transposition deficit of member states has steadily gone down until late 2009 and increased again a little by November 2011. What requires more explicit attention is the combination of a) a relatively high transposition deficit, b) a relatively high compliance deficit and c) a relatively high number of pending infringement cases. One option is to single out the worst-performing country at the end of the year (late 2011, Belgium), issue a special report and formulate a joint Commission/member state path towards better enforcement, for the sake of a better functioning internal market.

6. The partnership approach between the Commission and the member states, manifest in the pre-litigation stage (before a formal infringement procedure starts), is a success, as shown by EU Pilot. All member states should be incorporated in EU Pilot and cases referred from SOLVIT could be handled faster if the complementarity between SOLVIT and EU Pilot is clarified and if the analysis already made in SOLVIT is used in EU Pilot cases.

7. In the wider landscape of EU enforcement, 'preventive' approaches aim to reduce the likelihood that infringement might occur later. A considerable number of concrete successes in this new landscape demonstrate that this route is of great importance, although it seems to fall outside 'classical' enforcement concepts. We witness the increasingly active and positive involvement of member states in such approaches (in eight out of ten mechanisms). Major achievements include the mutual recognition Regulation 764/2008, the pro-active joint 'ownership' of the difficult implementation of the 2006/123 services Directive, the rapidly intensified and ever-more effective IMI (Internal Market Information) system of day-to-day inter-member states' administrative cooperation and the crucial cooperation of all member states in the 98/34 Committee preventing new technical barriers from arising in the internal market. These impressive examples underline, without any doubt, that preventive and cooperative approaches can be of great help in preventing enforcement problems. The EU should extend this form of cooperation wherever meaningful.

8. A much less-known preventive feature of (say) the last decade is the gradual shift from enacting directives to EU regulations. This trend also requires the active support of member states since, in quite a few instances,

they voluntarily forego the degrees of regulatory discretion that directives might still provide them with. EU regulations have, by definition, no implementation problems and application of EU law tends to be less of a problem, too. Moreover, EU regulations have the virtue of pre-empting regulatory heterogeneity between member states, which can be very costly for business operating throughout the single market. Where 'diversity', based on genuinely distinct preferences, between member states plays a role, EU regulations are not a good idea because the uniformity is likely to suppress such divergent preferences. However, in numerous more technical directives, heterogeneity arises from the fragmented national decision-making over 27 member states, which rarely has anything to do with distinct preferences, except the desire to make one's own laws. The huge shift in the internal market towards EU regulations over the last decade shows that member states have been prepared to dispense with a stream of directives (hence, with the transposition into domestic law) and enacting regulations instead, as a less cumbersome and clearer resolution of overcoming failures of the internal market. Member states are encouraged to continue with this trend in all cases where no distinct national preferences play a role and, in so doing, contribute directly to a lessening of enforcement problems.

9. In complex directives (such as the horizontal services Directive 2006/123), the partnership approach has proven to work very well. Rather than just waiting until an avalanche of implementation problems was bound to emerge, the Commission and member states have closely worked together in Brussels and in national capitals, as well as during the 'mutual evaluation' between EU countries' implementation, in order to realise a timely and reasonably homogeneous implementation, with only some exceptions. Of course, there are not many such complex directives. However, where they arise or have to be revised thoroughly, a joint 'ownership' of the implementation process should be repeated as this prevents many problems later.

10. The marvel of preventive approaches was and remains the 98/34 procedure, which aims at pre-empting the emergence of new technical barriers caused by new draft laws and decrees in member states. Our study provides empirical evidence supporting a slow but steady learning process in national administrations prompted by two and a half decades of notifications, and further disciplines following critical CJEU rulings. We also calculate the 'effective prevention rate' (of new technical barriers) for 2010 and 2011, which hovers around 10% of notifications. It is most likely that in the 1980s and 1990s, the prevention of new technical barriers has

been even more necessary (and empirical evidence suggests so much). Without 98/34, the internal goods market would simply have become a mockery: over the many years, probably thousands of new barriers have been pre-empted. The mechanism is intrusive if one holds a strict view of national parliamentary 'sovereignty', but in actual practice parliaments barely notice any restriction of their freedom to enact new technical laws (which of course cannot go against EU law anyway), yet the result of this procedure is very positive. Extending this type of procedure to some areas where the danger of undisciplined autonomy is significant is highly recommended. One possible example is in services falling under the horizontal services Directive 2006/123.

11. Of all areas where enforcement of EU directives is problematic, public procurement is undoubtedly the most difficult one. It is also a huge market, even when the thresholds for supplies and works are taken into account. In the past the regime suffered from serious implementation problems. The design of the EU public procurement regime hinges on the trade-off between the far-reaching demands to keep the system open, transparent and competitive, which leads to a lot of bureaucracy, and the costs and discouragement that such impositions give rise to for European business. This trade-off is never going to be resolved in a fully satisfactory manner, but there are signals that the preventive system errs by being too costly and cumbersome. It is also (too) prone to litigation. The heavy-handed bureaucracy might also lead public procurement to be 'static', avoiding innovation. Officials might often merely 'tick-off' a list of requirements, leading to weak procurement. Precisely, new bidders frequently come from across the border and might offer innovative variants. Less red tape and greater flexibility would almost certainly induce disproportionately higher interest from other EU countries, up from today's far too low cross-border award rates. These points lead us to strongly support the three draft Directives proposed in December 2011. This market has the potential to a) induce more cross-border competition and b) generate much higher 'welfare 'gains.

12. There are still numerous 'barriers', real and perceived, in the internal public procurement market. Member states have (too) much regulatory discretion because the procurement directives are 'coordination' directives, with insufficient harmonisation. The 'regulatory heterogeneity' in the area is far too costly for the businesses interested in cross-border or even EU-wide operation. More harmonisation and/or disciplines of national 'special or extra' rules and requirements should urgently be pursued. Also, the national review and remedies systems are vastly

different in terms of rules, procedures, ease-of-access and effectiveness. Such complications go squarely against the justified desire of business to have prior confidence in cross-border tenders. Quick access to national reviews of public procurement is an asset, but its utility is dramatically diminished by the overly fragmented arrangements that confuse business and undermine a level playing field. Harmonisation here is tough given the incorporation in national legal systems, but EU-wide performance criteria might be introduced to enhance confidence for cross-border entrepreneurs.

BIBLIOGRAPHY

Arnold, J., G. Nicoletti and S. Scarpetta (2011), "Regulation, resource allocation and productivity growth", EIB Papers, Vol. 16/1, European Investment Bank, Luxembourg.

Baldwin, Richard E. (2006), "The euro's trade effect", ECB Working Paper, No. 594, European Central Bank, Frankfurt.

Bardach, E. (1977), *The implementation game: what happens after a bill becomes a law*, Cambridge, MA: MIT Press.

Barnard, C. (2008), *The Substantive Law of the EU: The Four Freedoms*, 3rd edition, Oxford: Oxford University Press.

Barrett, S.M. (2004), "Implementation Studies: Time for a revival? Personal reflections on 20 years of implementation studies", *Public Administration*, 82, (2), June, pp. 249-262.

Boerzel (2001), "Non-Compliance in the European Union. Pathology or Statistical Artefact?", *Journal of European Public Policy*, 8 (5), pp. 803-824.

Boerzel (2002), "Non-State Actors and the Provision of Common Goods. Compliance with International Institutions", in Adriènne Héritier (ed.), *Common Goods: Reinventing European and International Governance*, Lanham, MD: Rowman & Littlefield, pp. 155-178.

Conway, P. and G. Nicoletti (2006), "Product market regulation in the non-manufacturing sectors of OECD countries: measurement and highlights", OECD Economics Department Working Paper No. 530, Organisation for Economic Co-operation and Development, Paris, 7 December.

Davidson, Lord Neil (2006), "Implementation of EU Legislation" (Davidson Review), November, London HMS (http://www.cabinetoffice.gov.uk/regulation/reviewing_regulation/davidson_review/index.asp).

Egan, M. (2011), "Single Market", in Eric Jones et al., *Handbook of EU Politics*, Oxford: Oxford University Press.

EU Court of Auditors (2010), "Impact assessments in the EU institutions: Do they support decision-making?", Special Report No. 3/2010, Brussels (http://eca.europa.eu/portal/pls/portal/docs/1/7912856.PDF).

European Business Test Panel (2009), Consultation on SOLVIT (ec.europa.eu/yourvoice/ebtp/consultations/2009/solvit/solvit_en.pdf).

European Parliament (2011), "Judicial training in the European Union Member States", Directorate General for Internal Policies, Legal Affairs Committee (http://www.europarl.europa.eu/committees/en/studiesdownload.html?languageDocument=EN&file=60091).

European Parliament (2011), "Cross-Border Alternative Dispute Resolution in the European Union", Internal Market and Consumer Protection, June (http://www.europarl.europa.eu/meetdocs/2009_2014/documents/imco/dv/adr_study_/adr_study_en.pdf).

Fabienne Ilzkovitz, Adrian Dierx and Nuno Sousa (2008), "An analysis of the possible causes of product market malfunctioning in the EU: First results for manufacturing and services sectors", *European Economy – Economic Papers 336*, Directorate General Economic and Monetary Affairs, European Commission.

Falkner, G. and O. Trieb (2008), "Three Worlds of compliance or Four? The EU-15 Compared to New Member States", *Journal of Common Market Studies*, Vol. 46, No 2, pp. 293-313.

Fritsch, O., C.M. Radaelli, L. Schrefler and A. Renda (2012), "Regulatory quality in the European Commission and the UK: Old questions and new findings", CEPS Policy Brief No. 362, CEPS, Brussels, January.

Graig, Paul and Gráinne de Burca (2009), *EU Law. Comments jurisprudence and doctrine*, Fourth Edition, Bucharest: Hamagiu Publishing House.

Guimaraes, H., A. Faria and M.J. Barbosa (2010), *Product -Market Integration: A Multi-Faceted Approach*, Bingley, UK: Emerald Publishers.

Hatzopoulos, V. (2008), "Legal aspects of the internal market for services", in J. Pelkmans, D. Hanf and M. Chang (eds), *The EU Internal Market in Comparative Perspective*, Brussels/New York: PIE Lang.

Ilzkovitz, F., A. Dierx, V. Kovacs and N. Sousa. (2007), "Steps towards a deeper economic integration: The internal market in the 21st century", *European Economy*, Economic Papers No. 271, January.

Kox, Henk L.M. and Arjan Lejour (2006), "Dynamic effects of European services liberalisation: More to be gained", MPRA Paper No. 3751, University Library of Munich, Germany.

Mastenbroek, E. (2005), "EU Compliance Still a Blackhole?", *Journal of European Public Policy*, 12(6), pp. 1103- 1120.

Mustilli, F. and J. Pelkmans (2012), "Securing EU Growth from Services", CEPS Special Report, CEPS, Brussels, October.

Nordås, Hildegunn Kyvik and Henk Kox (2009), "Quantifying Regulatory Barriers to Services Trade", OECD Trade Policy Working Paper No. 85, Organisation for Economic Co-operation and Development, Paris.

Ottaviano, Gianmarco and Paolo Ireo (2007), "Contract Enforcement, Comparative Advantage and Long-Run Growth", CEPR Discussion Paper No. 1419, Centre for Economic Policy Research, London.

Pelkmans, Jacques (2006), "Testing for subsidiarity", Bruges European Economic Policy Briefing (BEEP) No. 13, College of Europe, Bruges (http://www.coleurope.eu/sites/default/files/research-paper/beep13.pdf).

_____ (2007), "Mutual recognition in goods: On promises and disillusions", *Journal of European Public Policy*, No. 5, Vol. 14, August.

_____ (2012), "Mutual Recognition: rational, logic and application in the EU internal goods market", in Peter Behrens, Thomas Eger und Hans-Bernd Schafer (eds), *Okonomische Analyse des Europarechets*, Mohr Siebeck, Teubingen.

Pelkmans, J., E. Vos and L. Di Mauro (2000), "Reforming Product Regulation in the EU: A Painstaking, Iterative Two-Level Game", in Giampaolo Galli and Jacques Pelkmans (eds), *Regulatory Reform and Competitiveness in Europe*, Vol. I, Horizontal Issues, Cheltenham: Elgar.

Raustial, K. and A. Slaughter (2002), "International Law, International Relations and Compliance", *Princeton Law and Public Affairs Paper*, No. 02.2, The Handbook of International Relations, Sage Publications, Ltd.

Renda, A. (2011), *Law and Economics in the RIA World: Improving the use of economic analyses in public policy and legislation*, European Studies in Law and Economics, Intersentia.

Siedentopf, H. and J Ziller (eds) (1988), *Making European Policies Work: The Implementation of Community Legislation in the Member States*, London: Sage.

UNICE (2004), "It's the Internal Market Stupid! A company survey on trade barriers in the European Union", Brussels.

ANNEXES

Annex I. Breakdown by sector of the draft regulations notified by the member states of the EU in 2011, issued with a comment or a detailed opinion by the Commission or the member states

Sectors*	Countries																											
	BE	BG	CZ	CY	DK	DE	EE	EI	GR	ES	FR	IT	LV	LT	LU	HU	MT	NL	AT	PL	PT	RO	SI	SK	FI	SE	UK	TOTAL
Building and construction	0	1	0	0	1	11	0	1	1	3	6	0	0	3	0	0	0	2	6	0	0	2	0	3	2	1	3	46
Food and agricultural produce	4	0	1	1	5	1	3	1	4	3	7	6	3	0	0	5	0	3	1	1	1	0	2	4	7	0	4	67
Chemical	1	1	0	0	0	0	0	0	0	0	2	0	1	0	0	0	1	0	0	0	0	0	0	0	2	0	0	9
Pharmaceutical products	0	0	0	0	0	0	0	0	0	0	1	0	0	0	0	1	0	0	0	1	0	0	0	0	0	1	0	4
Domestic and leisure equipment	0	0	0	0	0	0	0	0	1	0	0	0	0	0	0	1	0	0	0	0	0	0	0	0	0	0	0	2
Mechanics	0	1	5	0	0	0	0	0	1	0	2	0	0	0	0	0	0	1	0	1	0	0	0	0	0	2	0	13
Energy, minerals, wood	1	0	0	0	0	0	0	0	0	0	1	0	0	0	0	0	0	0	0	1	0	0	0	0	0	0	0	3
Environment, packaging	2	0	1	0	1	2	0	0	1	0	2	4	1	0	0	1	0	1	0	0	0	0	0	0	0	0	3	19
Health, medical equipment	0	1	0	0	0	1	0	0	0	1	0	0	0	0	0	0	0	0	0	0	0	0	0	0	0	0	0	3
Transports	1	0	0	0	1	0	0	0	0	1	2	1	0	0	0	0	0	3	1	1	0	1	1	0	1	4	6	24
Telecommunications	0	0	0	0	0	4	1	2	0	8	2	0	0	0	3	0	0	1	1	0	0	1	0	1	1	0	2	27
Gambling, games of chance	0	1	1	0	0	2	1	0	1	5	0	0	0	0	0	0	0	0	1	0	0	0	0	0	0	0	0	12
Other products	0	1	1	0	0	0	0	0	0	0	0	1	0	0	0	2	0	0	1	0	1	0	0	1	2	1	2	13
Information society services	0	0	0	0	0	1	0	0	0	1	0	3	0	0	0	0	0	1	0	1	0	0	0	0	0	0	0	7
Total by member state	9	6	10	1	8	22	5	4	9	22	25	15	5	3	3	10	1	12	11	6	2	4	3	9	15	9	20	249

* For convenience, we have adopted the same categories of sectors used by the European Commission in its annual reports.

Annex II. Breakdown by sector of the draft regulations notified by the member states of the EU in 2010, issued with a comment or a detailed opinion by the Commission or the member states

Sectors	Countries																											TOTAL
	BE	BG	CZ	CY	DK	DE	EE	EI	GR	ES	FR	IT	LV	LT	LU	HU	MT	NL	AT	PL	PT	RO	SI	SK	FI	SE	UK	
Building and construction	1	0	0	0	0	7	0	0	0	1	1	1	0	2	1	0	0	0	3	2	0	0	0	0	2	0	1	22
Food and agricultural produce	3	2	2	2	5	3	1	1	0	12	7	4	6	1	0	1	1	2	0	2	1	1	1	3	0	6	0	67
Chemical	0	0	0	0	0	1	0	0	0	0	2	0	0	0	0	0	0	1	0	1	0	4	0	0	0	1	0	10
Pharmaceutical products	0	0	0	0	0	0	0	1	0	0	2	0	0	0	0	0	0	0	0	0	0	0	0	0	2	2	1	8
Domestic and leisure equipment	0	0	0	0	0	0	0	0	0	0	1	0	0	0	0	0	2	0	1	0	0	0	0	0	0	1	0	5
Mechanics	2	1	8	0	0	0	0	0	0	2	2	2	0	0	0	0	1	2	2	1	0	1	1	0	1	0	0	26
Energy, minerals, wood	0	0	2	0	0	1	1	0	2	0	0	0	0	0	0	0	1	0	0	1	0	2	1	0	0	0	0	11
Environment, packaging	1	0	1	0	0	0	1	3	0	1	0	0	1	0	0	0	0	0	1	1	0	0	0	0	1	0	0	11
Health, medical equipment	0	0	0	0	0	1	0	0	0	0	0	0	0	0	0	0	0	0	0	0	0	0	0	0	0	0	0	5
Transports	0	0	0	0	0	2	0	0	0	1	1	1	0	0	0	2	0	2	0	4	0	0	0	0	1	2	5	21
Telecommunications	0	0	0	0	2	0	1	0	0	0	3	1	1	2	1	0	0	0	0	1	1	4	0	0	1	0	2	20
Gambling, Games of chance	1	0	0	1	3	0	0	0	0	2	0	1	0	0	0	0	0	0	0	2	0	2	0	0	0	0	0	12
Other products	1	1	1	0	0	0	1	1	0	1	0	5	0	0	0	2	0	2	1	3	0	0	0	0	0	3	4	26
Information society services	0	0	0	1	0	1	0	0	0	0	5	3	0	0	0	0	0	0	0	0	0	0	0	0	1	0	1	12
Total by member state	9	4	14	4	10	16	5	6	2	20	24	18	8	5	2	5	5	9	8	18	2	14	3	3	9	15	14	256

Annex III. Detailed opinions issued by the Commission in 2010, following the notifications under Directive 98/34/EC *

No	Subject / Area	Sector	Comments	Problem type	Remedy
1	Honey & additives	Food and agricultural produce	No	Wrong implementation	Comply with Dir. & Regulation
2	Non-harmonised vessels	Transport	No	No mutual recognition clause	Insert mutual recognition clause
3	Tyre bales; end of the waste	Environment, packaging	No	Wrong implementation of the Directive; criteria lacking enforceability	Comply with the applicable concept/criteria laid down in the EU legislation
4	Labelling of construction products	Environment, packaging	Also	Additional requirements with the same effect as a quantitative restriction, without any justification	Remove the additional requirements
5	Marketing of very toxic, toxic or corrosive substances	Chemicals	Also	Non-compliance with the REACH Regulation and other directives; No notification of the dossier to the European Chemicals Agency	Comply with the REACH Regulation and remove restrictions not compatible with the relevant Directive
6	Ski helmets	Domestic and leisure equipments	No	EN standard mandatory	Insert equivalence clause
7	Pyrotechnical articles	Other products	Also	Infringement of the relevant EU Directive	Remove and adapt the provisions according to relevant EU Directive
8	Labelling of energy drinks with caffeine	Food and agricultural produce	No	Additional health warnings on energy drinks contain caffeine not in compliance with the Directive.	Elimination of the labelling requirement in order to comply with the relevant Directive
9	Medical devices, thermometers	Health, Medical equipment	Also	Making voluntary standards mandatory	Keep EN / other equiv. standards voluntary

10	Registration of food companies and foodstuffs	Food and agricultural products	Also	Non-compliance with the EU information and notification requirements established in the EU Regulation	Adapt the provisions/comply with the EU Regulation
11	Moist snuff and chewing tobacco	Other products	No	Improper implementation of the Directive(s)	Invitation to clarify certain points of the draft regulation and to abstain from adopting any measures that could jeopardise the objectives of the applicable Directive as well as those of food law
12	Wheelchair-accessible taxis	Transport	No	No mutual recognition clause	Insert a mutual recognition clause
13	Batteries and accumulators and related waste	Environment, packaging	No	Additional labelling requirements to those in the Directive, which fully harmonised the labelling, without recourse to the Art. 114 procedure	Elimination of the additional labelling requirements
14	Lifts	Mechanics	No	Additional requirements; making voluntary standards mandatory	Comply with new approach and this Directive
15	Driver location signs	Transport	No	No mutual recognition clause	Insert a mutual recognition clause
16	Portable traffic signal control equipment	Transport	Also	Proposed to allow for recognition of an equivalent standard where there is no adopted European standard; possible infringement Art. 34 and 36 TFEU	Take into consideration mutual recognition principle
17	Registration of poultry and ratities	Food and agricultural produce	Also	Requirements for the maintenance records for keepers of poultry are not in compliance with EU Directive	Adapt the provisions according to the EU Directive

18	Gambling games on the internet	Gambling, Games and related	Also	Restrictions that could infringe the freedom to provide services – Art. 56 TFEU	Adapt or remove provisions in conflict with the EU law
19	Mineral water	Food and agricultural produce	Also	Left out allowed additives; labelling too strict	Comply with 2 directives
20	Hot-water boilers, energy efficiency	Energy, minerals, woods	Also	The scope of the notified rules exceeds the scope of the relevant Directive	Reduce the scope of the draft regulation to align it with the relevant EU Directive
21	Food of animal origin, bee honey	Food and agricultural produce	Also	Scope/ details draft not in compliance with a Regulation	Reduce scope, alter specifics
22	Electronic cash registers	Mechanics	No	Additional requirements to those fixed in the EU Directives	Align the draft with the EU law, by guarantee that products bearing the CE marking will not be subject to additional requirements
23	Genetically modified organisms	Food and agricultural production	Also	Infringement of the EU Regulation; no compliance with the procedure laid down in the Regulation	Adapt the provisions/comply with the EU Regulation
24	Building products	Building and construction	No	Additional requirements for goods with CE mark without justification	Provision of reasons in public interest or removal of the additional requirements
25	Preparations classified as dangerous – toxicovigilance	Chemicals	Also	Draft not in compliance with the Directive	Align the draft with the EU law

26	Tourist railway vehicles	Transport	No	No evidence is given that the proposed measures are justified according to Art. 36 TFEU; No mutual recognition clause	Insert a mutual recognition clause
27	Devices for compliance with tyres	Mechanics	No	No mutual recognition clause	Insert mutual recognition clause
28	Road signalling panels, approvals	Transport	No	Additional requirements for goods with CE mark without justification	Provision of reasons in public interest or removal of the additional requirements
29	Products of animal origin	Food and agricultural produce	Also	The scope of the notified draft regulation goes beyond the scope of the applicable EU Regulation.	Reduce scope, remove conflicts with Regulation /Directive
30	Self-defence aerosol sprayers	Other products	No	Origin marking is forbidden	Replace origin marking by traceability requirements
31	Construction products	Building and construction products	No	No equivalence in several cases	Insert mutual recognition clause in several cases
32	Plastic films, on glazing	Building and construction	No	Mutual recognition clause drafted in very vague terms; double tests	Use standard mutual recognition; remove additional obligatory test
33	Marking on eggs	Food and agricultural produce	No	Wrong implementation of 2 Regulations	Adapt specifics of draft in order to comply with the EU Regulations
34	Devices measuring blood pressures	Health and medical equipment	Also	Making standards mandatory	Insert a mutual recognition clause
35	Fuels	Energy, minerals, wood	No	Restrictions to the free movement of goods without explaining why these measures are necessary and proportional – Arts 34 and 36	Elimination or justification of those measures

36	Pig carcasses	Food and agricultural produce	No	No compliance with the procedure and quantities lay down in the Regulation	Notify the Commission of maximum permitted number of slaughters, exempt from application of the Community scale
37	Genetically modified organisms	Food and agricultural production	Also	Infringement of the EU Regulation; no compliance with the procedure lay down in the Regulation	Adapt the provisions/comply with EU Regulation
38	Foodstuff, labelling, presentation and advertising	Food and agricultural products	Also	Non-compliance with labelling Directive and other Regulation	Remove and/or adapt the provisions in accordance with the EU Directive and Regs
39	Fixed storage tanks	Mechanics	Also	No mutual recognition clause	Insert a mutual recognition clause
40	Digital books	Information Society Services	No	Possible Restriction of the freedom of establishment (Art. 49 TFEU) and freedom to provide services + plus non-compliance with EU Directive	Adapt the provisions/comply with the EU Law
41	Breeding dogs	Other products	Also	No compliance with the EU regulation; extra-territorial application of national rules	Remove and adapt the provisions according to the EU Regulation
42	Tramways electrical systems	Transport	Also	No mutual recognition clause	Insert a mutual recognition clause
43	LED tube lights	Domestic and leisure equipments	No	Additional mandatory requirements, on the basis of their technical standards, contrary to the relevant Directive	Remove provisions conflicting with the relevant EU Directive

* In 2010, the European Commission issued a total of 44 detailed opinions, one of which was omitted in this table, because the case was reported to the Court of Justice of the European Union.